Drug
Control
and the
Courts

Drugs, Health, and Social Policy Series

Edited by James A. Inciardi
University of Delaware

About This Series . . .

The Sage **Drugs, Health, and Social Policy Series** provides students and professionals in the fields of substance abuse, AIDS, public health, and criminal justice access to current research, programs, and policy issues particular to their specialties. Each year, four new volumes will focus on a topic of national significance.

Drug Control and the Courts

James A. Inciardi
Duane C. McBride
James E. Rivers

Drugs, Health, and Social Policy Series
Volume 3

SAGE Publications
International Educational and Professional Publisher
Thousand Oaks   London   New Delhi

For information address:

SAGE Publications, Inc.
2455 Teller Road
Thousand Oaks, California 91320
E-mail: order@sagepub.com

SAGE Publications Ltd.
6 Bonhill Street
London EC2A 4PU
United Kingdom

SAGE Publications India Pvt. Ltd.
M-32 Market
Greater Kailash I
New Delhi 110 048 India

Printed in the United States of America

Library of Congress Cataloging-in-Publication Data

Inciardi, James A.
    Drug control and the courts / authors, James A. Inciardi, Duane C.
McBride, James E. Rivers.
        p.   cm.—(Drugs, health, and social policy series; 3)
    Includes bibliographical references and index.
    ISBN 0-8039-5476-X (Cloth: acid-free paper).—ISBN 0-8039-5477-8 (pbk.:
acid-free paper)
    1. Drug abuse and crime—United States.   2. Drug abuse—Treatment—
United States.   3. Drug abuse counseling—United States.
    4. Criminal justice, Administration of—United States.   I. McBride,
Duane C.   II. Rivers, James E.   III. Title.   IV. Series.
    HV5825.I538   1996
    354.2'4—dc20   95-50180

This book is printed on acid-free paper.

96   97   98   99   00   01   10   9   8   7   6   5   4   3   2   1

Sage Production Editor: Astrid Virding
Sage Typesetter: Andrea D. Swanson

Contents

Epidemiological data on drug use in the United States suggest two distinct patterns of involvement with cocaine, heroin, and other illegal substances. The first pattern occurs in the general population, that is, among the relatively stable "at home" residents who do not live on the streets or in jails, prisons, or other institutions. Among these individuals, existing data indicate that illegal drug use peaked around 1980, with noticeable declines in subsequent years, and a slight upturn in the 1990s.[1] For example, for high school seniors, 1979 was the peak year for the "annual prevalence" (any use during the past year) of both marijuana, at 51%, and any/all illegal drugs, at 54%. Since then, drug use rates have fluctuated in a downward trend, always remaining far below their earlier peak. Data from the National Household Survey indicate similar trends among adolescents and young adults. Combined, these data strongly indicate that among those in school as well as those living in stable households, illegal drug use has noticeably declined in recent years.

A very different pattern of drug use is apparent among criminal offenders, one involving increased drug use. Data from the Drug Use Forecasting (DUF) program indicate that in most of the monitored metropolitan areas, almost half of sampled felony arrestees tested positive for cocaine. Results in some urban areas—New York, Miami, Philadelphia, Washington, D.C., and Los Angeles—suggest that the arrestee population is virtually saturated with cocaine.

This high rate of cocaine use reflects a significant shift in drug use patterns among offenders. During the early 1970s, the relationship between drug use and crime was almost exclusively a problem of heroin use by street criminals. Research during those years indicated that between 15% and 40% of persons arrested or incarcerated were reporting heroin use, with only a small, scattered proportion reporting cocaine use. These reports caused the National Institute on Drug Abuse and the National Institute of Justice to organize a national panel to review the existing research on relationships between drug use and crime, and to suggest policies that might reduce the criminality of drug-using offenders. Heroin use and its relationship to property crime constituted the primary focus of both the existing research of that era and the considerations of the panel in 1975.

Thus, at a time when drug use is declining for students and those living in stable residential situations, street criminals have dramatically increased their drug use, and most of this increase involves cocaine—a drug clearly associated with violent aggressive behavior. These trends have created interest in new treatment initiatives for drug-abusing criminal offenders, especially because they have occurred simultaneously with three other factors bolstering interest in the wider use of drug abuse treatment.

First, prison populations started to grow dramatically at the beginning of the 1980s. State and federal prison populations grew by more than 100% from 1980 to 1990. At the close of the decade, state prisons housed a record 644,000 inmates, with federal prison inmates numbering some 56,500. By the mid-1990s, state and federal prison populations exceeded 1 million. These increases have been in great part a direct result of the "war on drugs." Thus drug use among street criminals continued to escalate even as more of them were being incarcerated, clearly suggesting that imprisonment alone is not an adequate solution to the drug problem. Further, the record numbers of inmates represent large financial burdens as states struggle to keep up with the problem.

Second, the spread of HIV and AIDS among drug users, and particularly among crack and injection drug users, is a large and growing problem. Because of the extensive involvement of drug users in criminal activity, and their consequent arrest and incarceration, the justice system is faced with the problem of screening and caring for an increasing proportion of offenders with HIV infection or those symptomatic for AIDS.

Third, the one helpful development is that recent research has convincingly documented the success of compulsory and coerced treatment for drug-involved offenders. Evaluation studies demonstrate that the key variable most related to success in treatment is *length of stay,* and that those coerced into treatment tend to remain longer than those voluntarily committed.

These assorted trends suggest a strong need for reexamination of the existing linkages between drug abuse treatment services and the criminal justice system, and particularly the courts, expansion of those linkages that have demonstrated effectiveness, and establishment of additional connections. Given this need, in this monograph we examine the history, development, and current status of programs of drug control linked to the American courthouse.

Note

1. The two major drug use monitoring systems are the National Household Survey and the National High School Senior Survey, both sponsored by the National Institute on Drug Abuse.

1. Drugs-Crime Linkages

For the better part of the twentieth century, there has been a seemingly endless controversy regarding the relationship between the use of illegal drugs (and specifically narcotics and cocaine) and criminal behavior. Representatives of the criminal justice system, the medical profession, and academia have reflected numerous points of view and have espoused widely differing reasons for their interest in the topic, and a detailed and focused analysis of the issues and the literature suggests that a whole variety of questions need to be addressed. For example, is criminal behavior, first of all, antecedent to addiction, or is the former a phenomenon that appears subsequent to the onset of addiction? More specifically, is crime the result of or a response to a special set of life circumstances brought about by addiction to illegal drugs, or is addiction per se a deviant tendency characteristic of individuals already prone to committing predatory crimes? Second, and assuming that criminality may indeed be a preaddiction phenomenon, does the onset of the chronic use of narcotics, cocaine, and/or other illicit drugs bring

1

about a change in the intensity and frequency of illegal acts? Does criminal involvement tend to increase or decrease subsequent to addiction? Finally, in what kinds of criminal offenses do addicts engage? Do they tend toward violent acts of aggression, are their crimes profit oriented and geared toward the violation of the sanctity of private property, or both?

To this subject, already belabored yet still inconclusively studied, one might also ask, is there any relationship at all between the two phenomena? Whatever the morass of studies may have concluded, can the derived relationships be attributed to differential police behavior, to defects in survey design, to purposeful or unintended bias, to the structure and functional application of laws circumscribing statuses characteristic of drug-using behaviors, or to a spectrum of changes that have occurred through time? Is our present state of knowledge, in the final analysis, no more than mythology or too fragmented for a composite picture?

Given all of the above, our purposes in this opening chapter are to review and analyze a number of the major research efforts that have been carried out in these areas of inquiry and to provide a framework for their interpretation. Furthermore, we offer commentary relative to some basic issues that must be addressed in the study of drug-taking and drug-seeking behaviors as they may relate to criminal activity and, ultimately, to their control by the courts.

The Criminal Model of Drug Abuse

Although the questions and issues surrounding the professed relationships between drug use and crime did not fully become a public debate until after the passage of the Harrison Narcotic Drug Act in 1914, a body of attitudes regarding users of narcotics had already evolved many decades prior to the onset of the 1900s. These became discussed more readily and with more hysteria when behaviors associated with drug taking and drug seeking ultimately became defined as criminal.

Opium had been utilized as a general remedy in this country as early as the settlement of colonial America, but the drug's availability on a large scale did not occur until its inclusion in numerous patent medicines during the nineteenth century. Opium and its derivatives had then become accessible to all levels of society and could be purchased over the counter in drug and grocery stores as well as through the mail. Remedies of this type were consumed for ailments of almost every type, from coughs to diarrhea, and had special favorability for the treatment of "female troubles."

Public concern regarding the "evil effects" attributed to opium, which contributed to the definition of its chronic use as a social problem, began to emerge shortly after mid-century. In 1856, for example, Dr. G. B. Wood (1856) dramatized the condition of chronic opium intoxication as being "evil," and suggested that indulgence in the use of the drug led to a loss of self-respect, that such usage represented the yielding of an individual to seductive pleasure, and that it was, in fact, a "vice." Dr. Samuel Collins (1887) further reiterated this point and estimated that perhaps hundreds of thousands of his fellow Americans were exposed to the "evil effects" of opium. Other observers, in contrast, described the affliction of opium use as a "disease." The vast numbers of Civil War veterans, for example, who had become addicted to morphine through its extensive intravenous administration for the relief of pain, were considered to be suffering from "army disease." The majority of such individuals were deemed "sick" rather than "deviant," and treatment in the form of medically supervised withdrawal was readily available in the offices of the men's family doctors.

By the close of the 1880s, however, the notion that addiction was evil seemed to be increasing, even among members of the medical profession. Dr. C. W. Earle, for example, expressed in the *Chicago Medical Review* the opinion that the opium habit, like the use of alcohol or gluttony, constituted a vice; similarly, John Shoemaker's 1908 edition of *Materia Medica and Therapeutics* reflected on "opium-eating" as a moral rather than a medical problem. Medical practitioners who supported the opinion that the user of opium was to be pitied rather than degraded, on the other hand, nevertheless contributed to an encompassing definition of the addict as someone quite divergent from the more "normal" members of the social mass. Constantin Schmitt, for example, suggested in 1889 that the condition was a psychophysical state; in 1894, Paul Sollier indicated that a neuropathic or psychopathic condition predisposed individuals to opiate addiction; and Wilson and Eshner's *American Textbook of Applied Therapeutics,* published in 1896, investigated the phenomenon in terms of a disease of both the body and the mind.[1]

To this collection of testimonials ascribing varying orders of stigma to the opiate user, a variety of authors added an alternative ethos as a possible arena for conceptualization and comment. With the view that "deviant" behavior—or even feeblemindedness, as Richard Dugdale (1877) had suggested in his well-known study *The*

Jukes—was biologically transmitted, addiction was deemed an unavoidable consequence of poor ancestry. Thompson (1902), an advocate of this notion, concluded that many addicts possessed a "strong neurotic inheritance," and indicated that the morphine taker might also indulge excessively in cocaine, chloral hydrate, opium smoking, absinthe drinking, or the use of alcohol in general.

In addition to drug dependence instigated through exposure to opium in patent medicines or by injectable morphine, public concern was also mounting relative to opium-smoking parlors. When gold was discovered in California in 1848, migrants from the Atlantic states as well as from Europe, Asia, and Australia contributed to the gold-seeking population. By 1852, some 27,000 Chinese immigrants had arrived on the California shores, and within two decades, their numbers exceeded 70,000. With them, the Chinese imported their cultural tradition of opium smoking, and they quickly established smoking parlors that were frequented by Asians and Americans as well (see Ashbury, 1933; Soulé, Gihan, & Nisbet, 1885).

With a Chinatown in New York City beginning in 1872, a city that was situated at the crossroads of the nation's publishing capitals, knowledge of the Chinese way of life and the practice of opium smoking became more readily disseminated. Further, a popular form of communication during that period were "antiurban" exposés, which took the form of lurid guidebooks that described the "evils" of the "great metropolis" of New York. Chinatown was a popular subject, and the customs of the celestials, as they were often called, as well as the "evil" nature of the opium "joints," were variously described (for example, see Buel, 1891; Campbell, Knox, & Byrnes, 1892; Crapsey, 1872; Knox, 1873; Lening, 1873; Martin, 1868; Smith, 1868).

Although the use of opium was not a crime during this period, the operation of opium parlors was illegal in New York City, and the suppressive activities of the police aimed at closing these establishments were readily included in the urban "guidebooks." Furthermore, descriptions of the opium habit and its consequences were dramatized as evil in police literature, and the behavior under observation was associated with criminality (for example, see Byrnes, 1895, pp. 39-40; Costello, 1885, pp. 516-524). Finally, by 1896 the term *dope fiend* had made its way into popular slang usage (Wentworth & Flexner, 1960, p. 181), implying that drug taking *was,* or at least resulted in, an evil obsession. By the end of the nineteenth century, cocaine and heroin had been added to the over-the-counter pharmacopoeia, creating ever greater concerns about drug "abuse."

The Harrison Act of 1914

It would appear that American drug policy originated from two competing models of addiction. As noted above, according to the *criminal model,* addiction was seen as one more of the many antisocial behaviors manifested by the growing classes of predatory and dangerous criminals. But there also was a *medical model,* in which addiction was considered to be a chronic and relapsing disease that should be addressed in the manner of other physical disorders—by the medical and other healing professions.

Many commentators have viewed the Harrison Act of 1914 as the ultimate triumph of the criminal model over the medical view, and as such, that single piece of legislation served to shape the direction of drug policy for years to come and generations yet unborn (see King, 1972, 1974; Lindesmith, 1965; Trebach, 1982). As Auburn University sociologist Charles E. Faupel (1991) has observed:

> The long-term result of this legislation was dramatic. Narcotics use was transformed from a relatively benign vice practiced by some of society's most respectable citizens to an openly disdained activity prohibited by law, relegating the narcotics user to pariah status in most communities. (p. 151)

Interestingly, however, history suggests a somewhat alternative story. Briefly, the Harrison Act required all people who imported, manufactured, produced, compounded, sold, dispensed, or otherwise distributed cocaine and opiate drugs to register with the Treasury Department, pay special taxes, and keep records of all transactions (see Walsh, 1981). As such, it was a revenue code designed to exercise some measure of public control over narcotics and other drugs. Certain provisions of the Harrison Act permitted physicians to prescribe, dispense, and administer narcotics to their patients for "legitimate medical purposes" and "in the course of professional practice." But how these two phrases were to be interpreted was another matter entirely.

On the one hand, the medical establishment held that addiction was a disease and that addicts were patients to whom drugs should be prescribed to alleviate the distress of withdrawal. On the other hand, the Treasury Department interpreted the Harrison Act to mean that a doctor's prescription for an addict was unlawful. The U.S. Supreme Court quickly laid the controversy to rest. In *Webb v. United States* (1919), the Court held that it was not legal for a physician to prescribe narcotic drugs to an addict-patient for the purpose of maintaining the patient's use and comfort. In *United States v. Behrman* (1922) the Court went one step further, by declaring that a narcotic prescription for an addict was unlawful, even if the drugs were prescribed as part of a "cure program." The impact of these decisions combined to make it almost impossible for addicts to obtain drugs legally. In 1925 the Supreme Court emphatically reversed itself in *Linder v. United States,* disavowing the *Behrman* opinion and holding that addicts were entitled to medical care as other patients were, but the ruling had almost no effect. By that time, physicians were unwilling to treat addicts under any circumstances, and well-developed illegal drug markets were catering to the needs of the addict population.

In retrospect, numerous commentators on the history of drug use in the United States have argued that the Harrison Act snatched addicts from legitimate society and forced them into the underworld. As attorney Rufus King (1974), a well-known chronicler of American narcotics legislation, has described it, "Exit the addict-patient, enter the addict-criminal" (p. 22). Or similarly:

> Drug abuse and drug addiction are social problems created largely by unenforceable laws and ineffective political bureaucracies. For example, in 1914 the Harrison Act was promulgated at the insistence of the Federal Narcotics Bureau. This Act, which defined all addicts as criminals and all physicians who prescribed opiates in treatment as law violators, was a significant contribution to making drug abuse and drug addiction socially created evils. (Brown, Mazze, & Glaser, 1974, p. xiii)

In counterpoint, however, the Federal Bureau of Narcotics had nothing to do with the passage of the Harrison Act of 1914, primarily because the agency was not established until 1930 (Anslinger & Tompkins, 1953, p. 117). More important, however, the Harrison Act did not instantly create a criminal class. Without question, at the beginning of the twentieth century most users of narcotics were members of legitimate society. In fact, the majority had first encountered the effects of narcotics through their family physicians or local pharmacists or grocers. Over-the-counter patent medicines and "home remedies" containing opium, morphine, and even heroin and cocaine had been available for years, and some even for decades (Inciardi, 1992b, pp. 2-11). In other words, addiction had been medically induced during the course of treatment for perceived ailments. Yet long before the Harrison Act had been passed, before

it had even been conceived, there were indications that this population of users had begun to shrink (Morgan, 1974). Agitation had
existed in both the medical and religious communities against the
haphazard use of narcotics, defining much of it as a moral disease
(see Terry & Pellens, 1928). For many, the sheer force of social
stigma and pressure served to alter their use of drugs. Similarly, the
decline of the patent medicine industry after the passage of the Pure
Food and Drug Act is believed to have substantially reduced the
number of narcotics and cocaine users (Courtwright, 1982). Moreover, by 1912, most state governments had enacted legislative
controls over the dispensing and sale of narcotics. Thus it is plausible
to assert that the size of the drug-using population had started to
decline years before the Harrison Act became the subject of Supreme
Court interpretation.

Even more important, however, are historical indications that a
well-developed subculture of criminal addicts had emerged many
years before the passage of the Harrison Act. By the 1880s, for
example, and as already noted, opium dens had become relatively
commonplace in New York and San Francisco, and the police
literature of the era indicates that they were populated not only with
"hopheads" (addicts), but with gamblers, prostitutes, and thieves as
well. As New York City Chief of Detectives Thomas Byrnes observed in 1886:

> The people who frequent these places are, with very few exceptions,
> thieves, sharpers and sporting men, and a few bad actors; the women,
> without exception, are immoral. No respectable woman ever entered one
> of these places, notwithstanding the reports to the contrary. The lan-
> guage used is of the coarsest kind, full of profanity and obscenity.
> (p. 385)

Importantly, the opium den, "dive," or "joint" was not only a
place for smoking, but a meeting place, a sanctuary. For members
of the underworld it was a place to gather in relative safety, to enjoy
a smoke (of opium, hashish, or tobacco) with friends and associates.
The autobiographies of pickpockets and other professional thieves
from generations ago note that by the turn of the twentieth century,
opium, morphine, heroin, and cocaine were in widespread use by all
manner of criminals (Black, 1927; Hapgood, 1903; Irwin, 1909;
Scott, 1916; White, 1907). And we might also point out here that
the first jail-based program for the treatment of heroin addiction
was established in the infamous New York Tombs (Manhattan City

Prison) 2 years before the Harrison Act went into effect (Lichtenstein, 1914). At the time, it was estimated that some 5% of the city's arrestees were addicted to narcotics. Finally, the involvement of criminal groups in subcultures of opiate and cocaine use went beyond the major urban areas, including numerous small cities as well (see Muth, 1902; Werner, 1909).

Thus, although the Harrison Act contributed to the criminalization of addiction, subcultures of criminal addicts had been accumulating for decades before its passage. Nevertheless, the Harrison Act was the first piece of *federal* antidrug legislation, and it carried with it the potential for application of the criminal label to addiction in a broader sense. Not only was the possession of narcotic drugs interpreted as a criminal offense, but the risk of arrest was also expanded in that the drugs became available only through nonlegal sources. Other lawbreaking as well, engaged in for the purpose of securing funds for the purchase of drugs, became more obvious.

As Kolb (1962, p. 16) indicates, the belief was widespread during the period shortly after the new drug law was enacted that 25% of all crimes were committed by addicts, and that such offenses were due to the alleged "maddening" effects of drugs. This latter notion, that addicts were prone to commit violent crimes, represented an initial stimulus for the ensuing discussions and debates relative to the relationship between drug addiction and crime.

Early Research Initiatives

Perhaps the first empirical effort on behalf of the drugs-crime linkage was undertaken by Sandoz (1922), who examined the drug-seeking behaviors of some 97 male and 33 female morphinists who passed through the Municipal Court of Boston in 1920. His conclusions suggest that the majority of the individuals studied had become criminal as a result of their addiction, but he clearly states as well that there were alternative types of addicts:

> An analysis of the arrest history of those addicts for whom the beginning of addiction is known shows that we have to deal with two sets of addicts, the first and distinctly larger, consisting of law-abiding individuals who have become criminals through the use of morphine, the second, of criminals who become morphinists. I believe this to be true, but less clear-cut than indicated by the figures, and that, in reality we have to deal with a series, the two ends of which correspond to the two sets in question. (p. 44)

Less than a half decade later, in an attempt to discount stereotypes associated with addiction, Kolb (1925) similarly noted distinctions among addicts. His analysis of 181 cases suggested that those addicts who were also habitual law violators tended to have been either *actual* or *potential* offenders prior to their addiction, and among a quantity of others, the offenses committed were principally for violations of the narcotics laws. Furthermore, an absence of aggressive crimes was generally characteristic of the criminal records of both groups studied.

Sandoz's and Kolb's analyses were the first to offer conclusions based upon concrete data, and in differentiating between the two sets of narcotics addicts, with their corresponding patterns of criminality, these authors provided a foundation upon which the crucial issues of the drugs and crime controversy were to evolve. Essentially, these issues involve four general ideologies:

1. that addicts ought to be the object of vigorous police activity because the majority are members of a criminal element and drug addiction is simply one of the later phases in their criminal careers;
2. that addicts prey upon legitimate society, and the effects of their drugs do indeed predispose them to serious criminal transgressions;
3. that addicts are essentially law-abiding citizens who are forced to steal in order to support their drug habits adequately; and
4. that addicts are not necessarily criminals, but they are forced to associate with an underworld element that tends to maintain control over the distribution of illicit drugs.

The notion that addicts ought to be the objects of vigorous police activity was a posture that was actively and relentlessly taken by the Federal Bureau of Narcotics and other law enforcement groups. Their argument was fixed on a notion of criminality, because their own observations suggested that the majority of the addicts they encountered were members of the underworld and addiction was simply a component of their criminal careers. In support of this view, an early report of the Bureau of Narcotics highlighted that the overwhelming majority of narcotics users indeed had criminal histories that preceded their careers in addiction by as much as 8 to 10 years (U.S. Treasury Department, 1940). Furthermore, the records of 119 trafficker-addicts were cited, indicating that 83% of the cases had criminal records prior to addiction, and similarly, "of one group of 225 criminal addicts studied by the United States Health Service, every one among them had committed a crime before the use of narcotics had begun" (U.S. Treasury Department, 1940, p. 23).

The position taken by the bureau was firm and unconditional. Addicts, it emphasized, represented a destructive force confronting the people of the United States, and whatever the sources of their addiction, they were members of a highly subversive and antisocial group. This approach did indeed have some basis in reality. Having been charged with the enforcement of a law that prohibited the possession, sale, and distribution of a commodity that was sought by perhaps millions of persons, the bureau's agents were confronted by addicts only under the most dangerous of circumstances. It was not uncommon for officers to be killed or wounded in arrest situations, and analyses of the criminal careers of many of the addicts apprehended suggested that the underworld was well represented among them (see Michelson, 1940).

By the 1950s, Harry J. Anslinger, then director of the Federal Bureau of Narcotics, had become the major spokesperson for law enforcement's interests in this controversy; his comments reflect the bureau's original position:

> The problem of narcotic drugs should be of vital interest to all law-enforcement officers. That crime and *narcotics* are interwoven is illustrated by the fact that violators of the narcotic laws head the list of all criminals in the United States having previous fingerprint records. This list includes persons convicted of offenses ranging from vagrancy to robbery, forgery, counterfeiting, burglary and other crimes. Of the narcotic law violators arrested during a recent year, 63 percent had previous records and arrests, whereas in the general arrests 42 percent of the persons arrested had previous fingerprint records. (Anslinger, 1951, p. 1)

Anslinger's testimony reinforced the notion of the "parasitic quality" of the addict, and as the addict was "a thief, a burglar, a robber; if a woman, a prostitute or a shoplifter," Anslinger contended that the long-term imprisonment of such individuals would rid the community of many a thief, and roundups of addicts represented one of the best ways of breaking up waves of pocket picking and burglary. In further support of the basic premise, it was noted that in Formosa, where opium was inexpensive, 70.8% of the opium makers nevertheless had prior criminal careers; in Canada more than 95% of the addicts were criminals; and in a U.S. survey of 1,268 narcotics violators, 67% of the addicts in the sample had previous records for other offenses (Anslinger & Tompkins, 1953).

While the Bureau of Narcotics (and now the Drug Enforcement Administration) remained silent on this issue in subsequent years, other police agencies continued to stress criminality in addiction. Joseph Coyle, a former commanding officer of the Narcotics Bureau of the New York City Police Department, demonstrated that of the 3,386 narcotics violators arrested in New York City during 1957, 84% had arrests for nonnarcotics violations prior to their first narcotics arrests (State of New York Joint Legislative Committee, n.d., p. 35). A few years later, Morgan (1965), formerly a narcotics detective and special agent of the Federal Bureau of Investigation, also indicted the addict population. In citing his analysis of 135 addict careers, he noted that 89% had criminal backgrounds; stressing that whereas *sick* people normally wish to be cured, he pointed out that *addicts* either failed to submit to treatment as would medical patients or they readily returned to their addicted state subsequent to "cure." Not unexpectedly, Morgan advocated a penal approach to addiction.

Other data offered by diverse empirical studies and independent research efforts also tended to support the position of law enforcement. A U.S. Department of Health, Education and Welfare (1963) report stated that most addicts committing serious offenses were previously criminal; 72% of 4,385 heroin users identified by the FBI had arrests for other criminal acts prior to their first narcotics arrests (President's Commission on Law Enforcement and Administration of Justice, 1967, p. 11); in New York State, 72% of 150 male addict-parolees studied were found to be criminal prior to their onset of drug use (Stanton, 1969, p. 12); and an analysis of the life histories of 169 Mexican Americans treated at the Clinical Research Centers of the National Institute of Mental Health (NIMH) at Lexington, Kentucky, and Fort Worth, Texas, found that 62% had criminal involvement prior to their addiction (Chambers, Cuskey, & Moffett, 1970). A study in support of this position involved interviews with 50 black addicts in the District of Columbia (Plair & Jackson, 1970). Although the inquiry was specifically directed to narcotics use and crime, the authors were not specific as to the actual crime-drugs sequence; they did state, however, that the "criminal activity appeared to be a part of the lifestyle of the addicts at the onset of addiction" (p. 16).

In a contrasting perspective, researchers and clinicians have offered data suggesting that in the majority of cases, criminal involvement occurs subsequent to the onset of addiction and that offense behavior represents the avenue by which individuals support their addiction to drugs. During the 1930s, Dai (1937) found that as many as 81% of 1,047 Chicago arrestees became criminal subsequent to addiction, and in the following decade, Pescor's (1943) study of 1,036 patients at Lexington found that 75% were addicts first (p. 43). Furthermore, Pescor's findings demonstrated that *records* of delinquency developed subsequent to addiction in 86% of the cases. In addition, the sequence of *addiction to crime* was found to be characteristic of 100% of the 137 Chinese addicts studied by Ball and Lau (1966, p. 70); 70% of the Lexington patients studied by DeFleur, Ball, and Snarr (1969, p. 228); 73% of the 94 addict-probationers treated at the Washington Heights Rehabilitation Center in New York City (Brill & Lieberman, 1970); and 63% of 266 Kentucky residents who were treated for narcotics addiction at the Clinical Research Center (O'Donnell, 1966, p. 376).

Contemporary Drugs-Crime Research

Among the difficulties reflected in the research from the 1920s through the 1960s is the static frame of reference in which addiction has been repeatedly perceived. Although Sandoz had reported differences among and within addict populations as early as the 1920s, a major portion of later efforts failed to address this phenomenon adequately. When the Federal Bureau of Narcotics began to call to the public's attention the idea that addicts should be considered members of the nation's criminal element, for example, their conclusions had some validity in terms of that segment of the addict population with which they had the most frequent contact. Primary among the directives of the bureau was the enforcement of the narcotics laws with respect to the importation of heroin from foreign ports; "traffickers" in narcotics were viewed as essentially different from most "users." Furthermore, that high rates of addiction were characteristic of some underworld cohorts during the first half of the twentieth century can be documented.

The vast body of literature describing the way of life of the professional criminal, for example, has documented the widespread use of opium and heroin among pickpockets, shoplifters, and other types of professional thieves. In addition to those professional offenders who, in their autobiographies, have made reference to their own use of narcotics, the high incidence of drug use among such thieves has been noted in numerous other sources (see Inciardi, 1975). More specifically, for example, May Churchill Sharpe (1928), an infamous operator of confidence and badger games on three continents during the early part of this century, has commented that

9 out of every 10 "crooks," during her period of exploit, were drug addicts (p. 13), and equally high rates of drug use have been described as characteristic of pickpockets. Maurer (1964) suggests that addiction among pickpockets was greater than in any other "racket," and pickpockets' spouses were often addicted as well. Finally, numerous authors have noted that many professional thieves resorted to drugs to relieve the pressures of their occupation, and that such drug use also was a manifestation of a thief's "loss of nerve." Criminologist Edwin H. Sutherland (1937), too, who provided the first comprehensive analysis of the social organization and occupational structure of the profession of theft, also commented on this relationship.

On the other hand, however, many of the comments offered by the Federal Bureau of Narcotics and other law enforcement bodies tended to be of a biased nature, and were often based on fallacious use of statistical data. Anslinger's characterization of the addict as not only a criminal but also vicious and reckless was a message directed to police agencies throughout the nation. The perception of the addict was limited to this context, and other behaviors common to individuals physically dependent on drugs were thus misinterpreted. Morgan (1965), for example, has implied that addicts' lack of interest in treatment, or their frequent relapses subsequent to detoxification, is sufficient to disqualify them from the category of the "sick," and hence they ought to be approached as criminals. Statistical data too have often been misinterpreted. For example, it was assumed that if an offender's official criminal history reflected arrests for nondrug violations prior in time to his or her first drug offense, the offender was invariably not considered an addict before such initial drug violations (see President's Commission on Law Enforcement and Administration of Justice, 1967, p. 11).

Although sample bias has tended to inhibit reliable generalizations from various law enforcement data, similar contamination has often emerged from data generated by serious researchers. Initially, addicts receiving inpatient care—arrestees, probationers, parolees, or inmates—typically represented the more dysfunctional members of the drug-using community in that their involvement was sufficient to bring them to official attention. In addition, many of the major studies were based at the NIMH Clinical Research Centers and involved large samples, but these were drawn from admission records for periods as long as 27 years. In such cases, the sample subjects were treated as a homogeneous unit and were rarely representative of the populations they were purported to typify. Samples have tended to be exceedingly small in many studies, and differences with respect to even the more common variables of age, sex, and ethnicity have not always been controlled for. Furthermore, given that the unreliability of official criminal statistics as a measure of the prevalence and incidence of particular behaviors has long since been documented, interpretations grounded in arrest data should be highly suspect. In an alternative direction, populations have been drawn for study from treatment settings with little account taken of the possibility of changing styles in addiction over time.

To recap, from the 1920s through the close of the 1960s, researchers conducted hundreds of studies of the relationship between crime and addiction (see Austin & Lettieri, 1976; Greenberg & Adler, 1974). Invariably, when one analysis would support the medical model, the next would affirm the view that addicts were criminals first, and that their drug use was but one more manifestation of their deviant lifestyle. In retrospect, the difficulties lay in the ways the studies had been conducted, with biases and deficiencies in research designs that rendered their findings of little value.

Research since the middle of the 1970s with active drug users in the streets of New York, Miami, Baltimore, and elsewhere has demonstrated that, at least with those drug users active in street subcultures, the medical model has little basis in reality (see Inciardi, 1986, pp. 115-143; Johnson et al., 1985; McBride & McCoy, 1982; Nurco, Ball, Shaffer, & Hanlon, 1985; Stephens & McBride, 1976). These studies of the criminal careers of heroin and other drug users have convincingly documented that whereas drug use tends to intensify and perpetuate criminal behavior, it usually is not the initiating factor in a criminal career. In fact, evidence suggests that among the majority of street drug users who are involved in crime, their criminal careers were well established prior to the onset of either narcotics or cocaine use. Thus it would appear that the inference of causality—that the high price of drugs on the black market per se causes crime—is simply not supported. On the other hand, these same studies suggest that *drugs drive crime* in that careers in drugs tend to intensify and perpetuate criminal careers.

Addiction and Social Marginality

Another view of the relationship between drug use and crime has been called the *ecological perspective*. Identified with the Chicago school of sociology of the 1920s, the ecological perspective implies that drug use and crime are statistically related because both behaviors occur in the same types of neighborhoods and both occur as the result of the existence of a common set of etiological variables. From this viewpoint, drug use does not directly cause criminality; rather, both behaviors are results of conditions and factors often placed under the heading of "social disorganization." These include high rates of poverty and unemployment, non-owner-occupied housing, and rapid demographic transition.

Within the ecological perspective, early studies of the prevalence of narcotics addiction in urban areas found the phenomenon to be concentrated in certain sections of the city (Faris & Dunham, 1939). Theory contemporary to that time conceived of the city as a series of concentric circles and zones, each containing divergent types of areas differentiated with respect to processes of urban expansion. Within the central portion of the city, high rates of social disorganization were observed to exist:

> Within the central business district or on an adjoining street is the "main stem" or "hobohemia," the teeming Rialto of the homeless migratory man of the Middle West. In the zone of deterioration encircling the central business section are always to be found the so-called "slums" and "badlands," with their submerged regions of poverty, degradation, and disease, and their underworlds of crime and vice. (Park, Burgess, & MacKenzie, 1925, p. 54-55)

A high incidence of drug addiction was readily observed in these centrally located, deteriorated sections, even in the pioneer studies in Chicago. Nels Anderson (1923) noted that many addicts were concentrated in the areas occupied by the hobo, tramp, and bum. Harvey Zorbaugh (1923) described the role played by drug addiction in the slum. Decades later, rates of addiction were still found to be highest in Chicago in those disadvantaged areas where the heaviest concentration of other types of social problems endured (Illinois Institute for Juvenile Research & the Chicago Area Project, 1953). Similarly, in an empirical study of the distribution of crime in Seattle in the 1950s, most narcotics law violators were found to reside in the city's central and most heavily deteriorated portions (Schmidt, 1960). Although recent research has set aside the concentric circle theory of urban structure, there is little argument that the highest concentrations of narcotics addiction and other social problems are to be found in the deteriorated "inner cities."

Some two decades ago, in what is now a relatively unknown and defunct drug journal, the relation between narcotics use and the presence of other social problems in inner cities was presented with some rather dramatic statistics (Inciardi, 1974). In 1969, researchers at the New York State Narcotic Addiction Control Commission compiled comprehensive statistical data on opiate use rates for New York City's 30 health center districts (aggregations of geographically and demographically contiguous census tracts). Each district was ranked in terms of its rate of opiate use as well as its rates of other social problems, such as poverty, financial assistance, unemployment, illegitimacy, and juvenile delinquency. The rates of opiate use for the 30 given areas were then correlated with the rankings of the statuses of other social problems. The results were some of the highest correlation coefficients ever encountered in social science research.[2] For example:

opiate use/poverty	$r = 0.92$
opiate use/unemployment	$r = 0.88$
opiate use/illegitimacy	$r = 0.81$
opiate use/financial assistance	$r = 0.78$
opiate use/delinquency	$r = 0.75$

It was clear from the data that opiate use was not causing poverty, unemployment, illegitimacy, financial assistance, and juvenile delinquency. Rather, the implication was that in those areas where opiate use rates were high, high rates of other social problems tended to exist side by side.

The argument being offered here is that drug use and crime tend to evolve contemporaneously among certain individuals residing in areas where rates of heroin, cocaine, crack, and other illegal drugs and criminal behavior are high; this was articulated most decisively by a 22-year-old heroin-using prostitute interviewed in Miami:

I've often thought that if I'd never started with the drugs I'd never had ended up turning tricks every day. But the more you make me think about it, the more I think that one had nothing to do with the other. You grow up in a place where everything is a real mess. Your father's a thief, your mother's a whore, your kid sister gets herself some new clothes by fucking the landlord's son, your brother's in the joint, your boyfriend gets shot tryin' to pull down a store, and everybody else around you is either smokin' dope, shooting stuff, taking pills, stealing with both hands, or workin' on their backs, or all of the above. All of a sudden you find that you're sweet sixteen and you're doin' the same things. I can't really say why I started stealing, using shit, and walking the streets. It all seemed to happen at once. It was all around me and it was an easy way out. It all came on kind of naturally. (quoted in Inciardi, 1986, p. 162)

Postscript

Many observers and researchers in the fields of both substance abuse and drug control have maintained that narcotics addicts are responsible for tens of millions of crimes each year in the United States. In addition, an unknown and perhaps greater number of crimes are committed by cocaine, crack, and other drug users. Contemporary data and analyses tend to support such contentions. Significant in this regard are the findings of the Drug Use Forecasting (DUF) program, which was established by the National Institute of Justice to measure the prevalence of drug use among those arrested for serious crimes (National Institute of Justice, 1988). Since 1986, the DUF program has used urinalysis to test samples of arrestees in selected major cities across the United States to determine recent drug use. Urine specimens are collected from arrestees anonymously and voluntarily, and then tested so as to detect the use of 10 different drugs, including cocaine, marijuana, PCP, methamphetamine, and heroin. What the DUF data have consistently demonstrated is that drug use is pervasive among those coming to the attention of the criminal justice system. Thus what all of this suggests is that the criminal justice system in general, and the courts in particular, may be the most appropriate place for addressing the drugs-crime linkage.

Notes

1. The works of Earle, Shoemaker, Schmitt, Sollier, Wilson and Eshner, and numerous others are cited and quoted in Terry and Pellens (1928, pp. 137-165).

2. For those unfamiliar with statistics of this type, the highest possible *r* value is 1.00, meaning a perfect correlation.

2. Legal Coercion and Drug Treatment

The use of legislative and judicial authority to coerce participation in drug treatment has only a short history in the United States (see Inciardi, 1992b; McBride & McCoy, 1993). Although the manufacture, distribution, and sale of alcohol has been either restricted or prohibited from time to time and place to place, the introduction of psychoactive drugs has occurred with minimal public reaction, and sometimes with considerable public enthusiasm. The nineteenth century saw the routinization of international trade routes and developments in chemistry that resulted in the introduction of ancient and newly refined drugs into the United States. Opium, morphine, coca, cocaine, and even heroin were often mixed with alcohol or other solvents and sold over the counter as "magical elixirs." There were no national and few local restrictions on their distribution or regulations on what could be offered to the public as "medicines."

Clearly, the law had a laissez-faire attitude toward the distribution of drugs. In fact, the manufacturers of over-the-counter patent

19

medicines were well integrated into the legitimate economic structure. In 1881, they organized themselves into the Proprietary Medicine Manufactures Association, and they successfully prevented regulation of their industry for decades. The claims of the drug purveyors that their potions had "magical" properties were never reviewed by private or government agencies. As David F. Musto (1973) notes, "Opiates and cocaine became popular—if unrecognized—items in the everyday life of Americans" (p. 3). Musto and other observers have concluded that at the beginning of the twentieth century, the United States was a fairly drugged society.

The laissez-faire nature of American drug policy began to change as the result of a series of reform movements that exposed the health and social risks associated with the chronic use of psychoactive drugs (Inciardi, 1992b). Among the earliest pieces of federal legislation introduced to deal with drug use was the Pure Food and Drug Act of 1906. It required manufacturers of over-the-counter medications to list the ingredients in their products. As a result, many of the preparations containing opiates and other drugs became less attractive to consumers and were eventually withdrawn from the marketplace. Shortly thereafter, conferences held in Shanghai in 1909 and the Hague in 1912 focused on the need for international agreements on effective drug policies. The specific purposes of these conferences were to examine the international trade in opium, to recognize the public health and behavioral consequences of opium use, and to reach international agreements regulating the opium trade. Grassroots support for drug regulation was also under way, often fed by media stories of the "evils" of narcotics use (Inciardi, 1992b). An outgrowth of these movements was the passage of the Harrison Act in 1914, which we have discussed in Chapter 1.

The Beginnings of Coerced Treatment

Although underworld drug cultures were well established prior to the passage of the Harrison Act, the new federal law increased the arrest and incarceration rates of drug users. Criminal justice systems in many jurisdictions were confronted with masses of new cases, and many courts and jails became severely overwhelmed (see King, 1974). In some locales, the federal government addressed this situation with a program of incarceration and compulsory treatment. Forced treatment was quickly challenged as unconstitutional, but the U.S. Supreme Court appeared to support the overall government initiative, establishing a climate in which such treatment could broadly evolve. In *Whipple v. Martinson* (1921), the Court held that within the framework of government responsibility for the public health and welfare, the state had a legitimate interest in regulating the use of "dangerous habit-forming drugs." More specifically, the defendant in *Whipple* was a physician who was convicted of furnishing drugs, out of his own drug supply, to a habitual user of narcotics. A Minnesota trial court determined that according to state statutes, it was unlawful for physicians to dispense certain narcotics to habitual users out of the physicians' own stocks. However, the defendant alleged that the laws of the state of Minnesota and the federal regulations of the Harrison Narcotic Drug Act of 1914 were in conflict. The Harrison Act assumed the authority for the regulation of the dispensing and prescription of drugs by physicians. For physicians to comply with the provisions of the act, they could dispense drugs only to patients under their medical or professional treatment and were required to maintain records of the drugs dispensed. It was a question of the good faith of the physician. In this case, did Dr. Whipple dispense the drug to a bona fide patient in the course of professional care?

The Minnesota statute differed from the Harrison Act in that (a) narcotic drugs could be prescribed only to addicts and (b) these drugs could not be given to habitual users from the physicians' own supplies. The Supreme Court affirmed the decision of the lower court in that, as construed, the Minnesota enactment did not interfere with the regulations of the Harrison Act. In effect, states could regulate the administration, sale, prescription, and use of dangerous, habit-forming narcotic drugs.

The following year, the decision in *United States v. Behrman* (1922), discussed briefly in Chapter 1, in many ways reaffirmed this position. In *Behrman,* a licensed physician prescribed 360 grains of morphine, 150 grains of heroin, and 210 grains of cocaine to Willie King, whom the physician knew to be an addict. King did not require the use of these drugs by reason of any disease or condition other than his addiction, and Dr. Behrman did not dispense these drugs for purposes of treating any ailment other than King's addiction. None of the drugs dispensed were administered to or consumed by King in the presence of the defendant. All of the drugs were given to King with the intention that they would be self-administered over a period of several days. Additionally, King was not restrained or prevented from disposing of the drugs in any manner that he so desired. The Supreme Court maintained that the manner and procedure by which the defendant prescribed these drugs was indeed in conflict with the stipulations of the Harrison Act.

The Court admitted that if a physician were to prescribe a single dose, or even a number of small doses, he or she would not likely be violating the act. However, this physician, by means of a prescription, enabled a known addict to obtain large quantities of drugs from a pharmacist. An ordinary dose of morphine is one-fifth of a grain; of cocaine, one-eighth to one-fourth of a grain; and of heroin, one-sixteenth to one-eighth of a grain—by these measurements, more than 3,000 ordinary doses were placed at King's discretion. Accordingly, the Court ruled that the physician's actions had breached the terms of the Harrison Act. Although *Behrman* related to a very specific case in which a single physician had prescribed large doses of narcotics, a widespread interpretation of the ruling was that a narcotic prescription for an addict was unlawful, even if it was part of a legitimate treatment regimen.

Three years later, the *Behrman* decision was reversed through the Supreme Court's finding in *Linder v. United States* (1925). In *Linder,* a licensed physician was charged with knowingly, willfully, and unlawfully giving Ida Casey one tablet of morphine and three cocaine tablets. Casey was known by the defendant to be a habitual user of morphine and cocaine and to have no other diseases or conditions requiring the administration of these drugs. Dr. Linder did not administer the drugs, nor were they consumed in his presence. It was the doctor's intention that Casey would self-administer the drugs, but there were no restraints on how she could dispose of them. The trial court asserted that if Dr. Linder did, in fact, know that Casey was an addict and he dispensed these drugs for purposes of satisfying her cravings for the drugs, then he was guilty. But if the defendant in good faith prescribed the drugs to relieve pain from some other ailment, then he was not guilty. However, the Supreme Court decided that the physician acted within the scope of the Harrison Act and that it was within the course of a medical practice for a physician to provide relief from suffering, even if the patient is suffering only because he or she is a habitual drug user. The Harrison Act, the Court continued, said nothing of "addicts" and did not endeavor to impose methods for their medical treatment. The Court pointed out that in *Behrman* the physician was at fault only for prescribing such enormous quantities of drugs, thus Dr. Linder, a physician who acted according to fair medical standards, was proper in giving an addict a moderate amount of drugs in order to relieve conditions incident to addiction. It is interesting that, despite the Court's careful wording, federal, state, and local jurisdictions largely ignored the *Linder* ruling, and continued to follow the earlier rulings in *Whipple* and *Behrman.*

During the 1920s and 1930s, strong antidrug sentiments flooded the national media, which continuously described the horrific and violent results of the use of "narcotics."[1] For example, Captain Richmond P. Hobson, one of the most celebrated heroes of the Spanish-American War, spoke against the "drug menace" in regular national radio broadcasts and wrote about it in articles published in monthly news and literary magazines. He popularized the notion that addicts were "beasts" and "monsters," and argued that narcotics could usher in an end to civilization (Hobson, 1928). The national press, including the prestigious *New York Times,* carried lurid stories about the consequences of drug use, and government-produced educational materials also argued that opiates and marijuana were the major causes of violence in U.S. society. In the 1930s, Harry J. Anslinger entered the picture. As the head of the federal antinarcotics establishment, he portrayed drug users as diabolical murderers and rapists, and in his crusade against marijuana, he was joined by Captain Hobson (Anslinger & Tompkins, 1953). Not surprisingly, the coalescence of media, government, and other antidrug efforts had a dramatic impact on the numbers of drug-involved offenders coming to the attention of the criminal justice and human services delivery systems.

As state and federal prison officials found themselves confronted with growing numbers of drug-involved inmates, they also realized that they faced the responsibility of addressing these new prisoners' medical needs. Among the more common treatment procedures was the "Lambert-Towne" method (see Nellans & Massee, 1928), which involved the withholding of the drug to which the patient was addicted, thus producing rapid withdrawal. The discomfort and medical dangers of withdrawal were ameliorated through doses of tincture of belladonna, fluid extract of xanthoxylum, and hyoscyamus.[2] Strychnine and digitalis also were used if necessary to improve blood circulation.

In reaction to the thousands of individual addicts who were being incarcerated in federal institutions, in 1929 the U.S. Congress passed the Porter Narcotic Farm Act. This new law authorized the establishment of what came to be called narcotics farms or narcotics hospitals. It was thought that institutionalizing addicts in specialized treatment facilities would help to unclog courts and prisons and make it easier to provide the medical care the addicts needed. Two facilities were established, one in Lexington, Kentucky, in 1935 and the other in Fort Worth, Texas, in 1938. These institutions were to provide clinical treatment for both federal prisoners and voluntary admissions. Although it appears that most of those treated were classified as volunteer patients, many were under considerable legal pressure to enter treatment (see O'Donnell, 1969).

Alternatively referred to as narcotics farms (because some addict-patients did farm work while in treatment), narcotics hospitals, and Public Health Service hospitals, for the next three decades these two institutions provided treatment services to thousands of addict-patients. In addition, they exemplified the national policy of using federal law and judicial processing to require individuals to receive treatment. Moreover, because of the large numbers of addicts sent to these facilities, clinicians and researchers interested in studying and treating drug abuse were drawn to Lexington and Fort Worth. The federal government also established relatively well funded research units at the facilities. As a result, from their establishment through the 1970s, significant numbers of the drug abuse clinicians and researchers in the United States were trained and/or worked at these hospitals (Ball & Chambers, 1970; Maddux, 1978).

Criminal Justice Diversion and Coerced Treatment

Criminal justice diversion refers to the removal of offenders from the application of the criminal law at any stage of the police and court processes (McBride, 1978, p. 246). It implies the formal halting or suspension of traditional criminal proceedings against persons who have violated criminal statutes in favor of processing them through some noncriminal disposition or means. Thus diversion occurs prior to adjudication; it is a preadjudication disposition.

The Development of Diversion

Diversion is not a new practice in the administration of justice. It has likely existed in an informal fashion for thousands of years, since the inception of organized law enforcement and social control. In ancient and modern societies, informal diversion has occurred in many ways: A police officer removes a public drunk from the street and takes him to a Salvation Army shelter; a state attorney decides not to prosecute a petty thief; a magistrate releases with a lecture an individual who assaulted a neighbor during the course of an argument. These are generally discretionary decisions, undertaken at random and off the record, and they tend to be personalized, standardless, and inconsistent. They are often problematic in that they may reflect individual, class, or social prejudices. Furthermore, they serve only to remove offenders from the application of criminal penalties, with no attempt to provide appropriate jurisprudential alternatives.

Although these haphazard and unsystematic practices will continue, more formalized diversion activities impose social-therapeutic programs in lieu of conviction and punishment. This form of diversion seems to have emerged within the juvenile justice system during the early part of the twentieth century. Among the first was the Chicago Boys' Court, founded in 1914 as an extralegal form of probation. As explained many years ago by Chicago municipal court judge Jacob Braude (1948), the rationale of the Boys' Court was to process and treat young offenders without branding them as criminals:

> While the facility of probation is available to court, it is used at a minimum because before one can be admitted to probation he must first be found guilty. Having been found guilty, he is stamped with a criminal record and then telling him to go out and make good is more likely to be a handicap than an order. (p. 12)

The Boys' Court system of supervision placed each young defendant under the authority of one of four community agencies: the Holy Name Society, the Chicago Church Federation, the Jewish Social Service Bureau, or the Colored Big Brothers. After a time, the court requested a report on the defendant's activities and adjustment, and if the report was favorable, he would be officially discharged from the court with no criminal record.

Later developments in youthful diversionary programs included New York City's Youth Counsel Bureau, which was established during the early 1950s to handle juveniles alleged to be delinquent or criminal (including drug offenders) but not deemed sufficiently advanced in their misbehavior to be adjudicated and committed by the courts (Glaser, Inciardi, & Babst, 1969). Referrals came from police, courts, schools, and other sources. The bureau provided counseling services and discharged those whose adjustment appeared promising. In many instances, the youthful defendants avoided not only criminal convictions but arrest records as well. Alternative programs in the developing area of juvenile diversion included the

District of Columbia's Project Crossroads, which was aimed at unemployed and underemployed first offenders ages 16 to 25 who were charged with property offenses (Leiberg, 1971). Upon agreement to enter the program, a youth's charge was suspended for 90 days, during which counseling, education, and employment services were made available to him or her. At the end of the 90 days, project staff would recommend that charges be dropped, that the youth receive further treatment, or that the youth return to the court for resumption of prosecution.

Patterns of Diversion

As criminal justice diversion continued to evolve, the arguments in its favor increased. It was felt that its practice would reduce court backlogs, provide early intervention before the development of full-fledged criminal careers, ensure some consistency in selective law enforcement, reduce the costs of criminal processing, and enhance offenders' chances for community reintegration. More important, however, was the conclusion reached by many social scientists and penal reformers that the criminal justice process, which was designed to protect society from criminals, often contributed to the very behavior it was trying to eliminate. This was typically accomplished in the following ways:

1. It forced those convicted of criminal offenses to interact with other, perhaps more experienced, criminals, and thus to become socialized in a variety of criminal roles, learning the required skills and the criminal value system.
2. It denied convicted felons the opportunity to play legitimate roles.
3. It changed the individual's self-concept to that of a criminal. This occurred as a result of a person's being told by the courts that he or she was a criminal and being placed in an institution where inmates and guards also defined him or her as a criminal (McBride, 1978).

Both the President's Commission on Law Enforcement and Administration of Justice in 1967 and the National Advisory Commission on Criminal Justice Standards and Goals in 1973 heavily endorsed the diversion concept, holding that it would not only offer a viable alternative to incarceration, but also minimize the potential criminal socialization and labeling of first offenders. Primarily as a result of massive federal funding allocated by the Law Enforcement Assistance Administration for the prevention and reduction of crime, diversion programs of many types emerged and expanded throughout the nation during the 1970s. Most, however, were designed for youths, for minor crimes (such as assaults, simple thefts, and property damage resulting from neighborhood disputes), and for special offenders whose crimes were deemed to be related to problem drinking or drug abuse. Some examples are presented below.

Youth service bureaus. Specifically recommended by the President's Commission and begun in California during 1971, youth service bureaus became common by the mid-1970s. They were similar in concept to New York's original Youth Counsel Bureau, but many operated as adjuncts to local police departments. They offered counseling, tutoring, crisis intervention, job assistance, and guidance with school and family problems for truants, runaways, and delinquent youths.

Public inebriate programs. In municipalities where public intoxication has remained a criminal offense, several diversionary alternatives to prosecution have been structured for public inebriates. Some are placed in alcohol detoxification centers rather than in jails. Others are referred before trial to community service agencies for more intensive treatment and care.

Civil commitment. Based on a medical model of rehabilitation, civil commitment programs were founded on the notion that some types of criminality result from symptoms of illness rather than malicious intent. Such offenders as drug users, sexual deviants, and the mentally ill could be diverted either before or after trial to a residential setting for therapeutic treatment. Community protection was promised by the removal of offenders to rehabilitation centers, and those diverted received treatment instead of criminal sanctions and stigma. Civil commitment programs were most common in California, New York, and the federal system for the treatment of drug abusers. (Civil commitment is discussed in greater detail below.)

Treatment Alternatives to Street Crime. Treatment Alternatives to Street Crime, better known as TASC, is a program designed to serve as a liaison between the criminal justice system and community treatment programs. As a program for substance-abusing arrestees, probationers, and parolees, its more than 120 sites in 25 states make it the most widely supported form of court diversion in the United States. (TASC is discussed at length in Chapter 3.)

Civil Commitment

Many states and municipalities had been sending drug-involved offenders to Lexington and Fort Worth since the late 1930s. However, the large numbers of addicts in New York and California, and the cost and inconvenience of sending probationers, prisoners, and parolees so far away, encouraged these and other jurisdictions to develop their own alternatives. The major initiative that began in the 1960s was the use of civil law to coerce drug addicts into treatment. This represented a considerable departure from the more traditional mechanisms of coerced treatment—in lieu of imprisonment, as a condition of probation or parole, or as a part of an offender's sentence.

At the time, civil commitment for the treatment of mental illness had long standing in civil law. As noted by British scholars, there is a common-law tradition arguing that society has the right to treat forcefully those whose behaviors represent danger to others (Council for Science and Society, 1981).

The theory of civil commitment in the United States holds that some drug abusers are motivated to obtain treatment, but most are not. As such, there must be some lever for diverting into treatment those who ordinarily would not voluntarily seek help (Inciardi, 1988). This lever has been referred to in the literature as "rational authority" (Brill & Lieberman, 1970; Meiselas & Brill, 1974)—a late-1960s euphemism for *not necessarily punitive* but nevertheless *mandatory* treatment.

Guided by this philosophy, as well as by fears of growing rates of drug-related street crime and public demands to "get addicts off the streets," a series of new programs were established based on the rational authority design. The first was in California in 1962. Known as the California Civil Addict Program, it was a large civil commitment initiative under which addict-patients could be institutionalized for up to 7 years without first being convicted of any criminal offense.

Robinson v. California

A major impetus for the expansion of civil commitment and other forms of coerced treatment came in the aftermath of *Robinson v. California,* decided by the U.S. Supreme Court in 1962. The case involved a petitioner's appeal of his conviction as a narcotic addict under a section of the California Health and Safety Code that read:

No person shall use, or be under the influence of, or be addicted to the use of narcotics, excepting when administered by or under the direct supervision of a person licensed by the State to prescribe and administer narcotics. It shall be the burden of the State to show that it comes within the exception. Any person convicted of violating any provision of this section is guilty of a misdemeanor and shall be sentenced to serve a term of not less than 90 days nor more than a year in the county jail.

The Supreme Court reversed Robinson's conviction, declaring that status offenses such as "being addicted to narcotic drugs" are unconstitutional, and that imprisonment for such an offense violates the Eighth Amendment ban against cruel and unusual punishment. Although *Robinson* dealt primarily with an Eighth Amendment issue, a lesser-known part of the ruling concerned a state's right to establish a program of compulsory treatment for narcotics addiction. Further, the Court ruled that such treatment could involve periods of involuntary confinement, with penal sanctions for failure to comply with compulsory treatment procedures. Largely as a result of the *Robinson* decision, New York and Massachusetts established civil commitment programs within the next few years, with other states following during the subsequent decade.

The Narcotic Addict Rehabilitation Act

In 1963, President John F. Kennedy convened a special conference on drug abuse in which there was considerable advocacy and support for coerced treatment in general and civil commitment in particular (Petersen, 1974). As a result of this meeting, the 1963 President's Advisory Commission on Narcotic and Drug Abuse recommended that a federal civil commitment law be enacted to provide for a civil alternative to treatment coercion through the criminal law. In 1966, Congress passed Public Law 89-793, better known as the Narcotic Addict Rehabilitation Act (NARA).

There were four titles or elements to NARA that served to both broaden and systematize national policy on compulsory treatment. Title I allowed for the *diversion* of addicts charged with federal crimes to treatment in lieu of prosecution. There were restrictions on who was eligible, for the program was designed primarily for nonviolent offenders. The surgeon general was authorized under Title I to place such offenders into treatment for up to 36 months. Title II of the act allowed the U.S. attorney general to "commit" addicts convicted of federal offenses "to residential treatment instead of jail or prison for a time not to exceed 10 years." NARA's Title III was apparently meant to be the federal companion to the civil commitment laws emerging in many states, and allowed for the "civil commitment of addicts to institutional treatment." The addicts themselves or individuals closely related to them could petition the local U.S. attorney for their commitment to treatment. The maximum time allowable for institutional treatment under Title III was 6 months, followed by up to 36 months of aftercare. Title III also allowed for 6 months of reinstitutionalization, if required, during the aftercare period. More than 90% of the admissions to the federal treatment hospitals at Lexington and Fort Worth in the last years of their operation were NARA Title III patients (Maddux, 1988, pp. 35-56). Because the period of confinement under Title III was only 6 months, it was often preferred by addicts as a means of rapid-turnaround treatment with community aftercare. In addition, Title III was often used as a condition of probation. Title IV authorized the creation and funding of community aftercare facilities.

Taken together, NARA's four titles provided the framework for a fairly comprehensive national policy for criminal and civil court coercion of drug abusers into treatment. Although by 1974 the federal narcotics facilities at Lexington and Fort Worth had ceased functioning as civil commitment hospitals and became prisons, coerced treatment and the assumptions underlying the Narcotic Addict Rehabilitation Act continued at the state level and in many ways continued to provide the rationale for new directions in national policy.

Postscript

It is difficult to assess the overall value and impact of the national diversion and civil commitment efforts. Many programs have never been evaluated, and estimations of their effectiveness have been based on little more than clinical intuition and hunches. Among those that have undergone rigorous assessment, the findings have ranged from promising to bleak.

On the positive side, however, many of the early diversion programs seemed to be effecting measurable change with certain defendants. An example is the Manhattan Court Employment Project, which was operated by New York's Vera Institute of Justice from 1967 through 1970. Its focus was on both male and female offenders charged with misdemeanors and minor felonies. Clients were given job training and placement, and those who failed to show any progress were returned to the courts for prosecution. An evaluation in 1972 demonstrated that the recidivism rate among defendants whose charges were dropped was half that of the defendants returned for prosecution (Manhattan Court Employment Project, 1972).

Conversely, the experiences of the youth service bureaus were considerably less impressive. Although the bureaus were touted as models for diverting many drug-involved juveniles from the criminal justice system, a national assessment of the projects found that they contributed little to any community in helping solve the problem of youth crime (Schechter & Polk, 1977).

The concept of pretrial diversion continued through the 1980s, but with somewhat less enthusiasm. Despite the problematic character of many of the programs, a few new and innovative operations nevertheless emerged. A striking example is the Weekend Intervention Program (WIP) in Dayton, Ohio. Begun in 1978 and sponsored by the Wright State University School of Medicine, the WIP was structured in response to growing concern over drunk drivers. First and second DWI (driving while intoxicated) offenders are given the option of conviction and sentence or a 3-day program of intensive therapy and alcohol education. Persons diverted to the WIP pay a fee for the services provided, making the operation self-supporting.

In 1983, the National Highway Traffic Safety Administration supported an evaluation of the WIP (see National Highway Traffic Safety Administration, 1985). The research identified, from court dockets, virtually every alcohol-related vehicular conviction in a 10-county area in southwestern Ohio. These cases, almost 6,000 of them, were followed for a 2-year period. The research compared the rates of repeated DWI offenses among three groups of convicted offenders: those who were sentenced to jail for 2 or 3 days, those who received suspended sentences or fines, and those who were remanded to Wright State's Weekend Intervention Program. It was found that the rate of repeated DWI offenses among first-time offenders was 7% lower for those sent to the WIP than for those receiving jail sentences or suspended sentences/fines. Moreover, among more serious drunk driving cases—those involving drivers with prior DWI convictions—the repeat offense rate for drivers sent to the WIP was 22% lower than the rate for drivers receiving jail or suspended sentences.

As jail and prison populations have continued to grow well beyond capacity in the 1990s, diversion programs have remained popular because they permit judges to impose intermediate sanctions yet still avoid incarcerating offenders—and the great majority of these offenders are drug involved.

As for civil commitment, there are extensive data on the effectiveness of the California Civil Addict Program (Anglin, 1988; McGlothlin, Anglin, & Wilson, 1977). Interestingly, because of procedural difficulties in the implementation of the program, comparison groups equivalent to the treatment cohort naturally emerged, composed of (a) those who were qualified for the program but did not enter and (b) those who were admitted but were immediately discharged because of questions of legality of the commitment procedures. All of the groups were followed. The research found that whereas the comparison and civil commitment treatment groups were equivalent in levels of criminal behavior and drug use prior to the initiation of the program, in 10 or more years after treatment the civil commitment clients had committed fewer crimes, spent less time incarcerated, and were less likely to use drugs than were those in the comparison groups. One conclusion was that "civil commitment and other legally coercive measures are useful and provided strategies to get people into a treatment program when they will not enter voluntarily" (Anglin, 1988, p. 31).

By contrast, the civil commitment program in New York has been judged to be an abject failure. The New York program was poorly designed, staff were improperly selected and trained, and, in general, treatment and administrative operations were mismanaged and misrepresented (Inciardi, 1988). Moreover, a report by the New York City Health Policy Advisory Center in 1967 found that the program—officially known as the Narcotic Addiction Control Commission (NACC)—was rife with brutality, offered limited services, and provided treatment in an oppressive, prisonlike atmosphere that resulted in high rates of escape and absconding. By the early 1970s, the program quietly died.

The NARA initiative appeared to be far better organized and implemented than the New York experience, but evaluations of the programs at Lexington and Fort Worth were not overwhelmingly positive. Stephens and Cottrell (1972) found that almost two-thirds of their follow-up study population became readdicted to drugs within 6 months after discharge, and only some 13% had avoided the use of any opiates during that same period.

Finally, a few researchers and clinicians began arguing that for treatment to be effective, clients had to see their need for treatment. From this perspective, treatment would work only if clients had experienced the consequences of their addiction and concluded that they voluntary wanted, and were ready for, treatment. According to this thinking, treatment would not work if there was external legal pressure for treatment participation. Coercive programs were seen as violating the basic understandings and principles of the therapeutic process. Stephens (1987) has argued that coerced treatment is not based on solid clinical theory, that it may be a violation of a patient's civil rights, and that it simply has not worked. But in counterpoint, and as we discuss at length in Chapter 3, evaluations of the Treatment Alternatives to Street Crime initiative of the 1970s, 1980s, and 1990s have been far more positive. Moreover, other studies have demonstrated that coerced treatment can work as well as, and perhaps better than, voluntary treatment.

Notes

1. It should be noted that at that time cocaine and marijuana (which are not narcotics) were included in the category of narcotics along with opium, morphine, and heroin (which are narcotics).

2. Xanthoxylum is a preparation made from the dried bark and berries of the xanthoxylum tree, which grows in the United States south of Virginia. It has been used to ease toothache and to soothe stomach pain. Hyoscyamus, also known as henbane or hog's bean, comes from the leaves and flowering tops of *Hyoscyamus niger*. Its active ingredient is scopolamine, which, among other things, is an antispasmodic.

3. Treatment Alternatives to Street Crime

The early 1970s witnessed the initiation of federal and community cooperation in a variety of areas. In the arena of substance abuse treatment, the federal government closed the narcotics hospitals and shifted resources and attention to funding local community efforts directly. With this framework, federal funds were used to launch a major new partnership between local courts and community drug treatment—the Treatment Alternatives to Street Crime (TASC) program under the auspices of the Law Enforcement Assistance Administration (LEAA).

Treatment Alternatives to Street Crime currently represents the oldest and most systematized linkage between drug abuse treatment and American courts. TASC provides an objective bridge between two separate institutions: the criminal justice system and the drug treatment community. The justice system's legal sanctions reflect concerns for public safety and punishment, whereas treatment emphasizes therapeutic intervention as a means for altering drug-taking and drug-seeking behaviors.

Under TASC, community-based supervision is made available to drug-involved individuals who would otherwise burden the justice system with their persistent drug-associated criminality. More specifically, TASC identifies, assesses, and refers drug-involved offenders to community treatment services as an *alternative* or *supplement* to existing justice system sanctions and procedures. In the more than 100 jurisdictions where TASC currently operates, it serves as a court diversion mechanism or a supplement to probation supervision. After referral to community-based treatment, TASC monitors the client's progress and compliance, including expectations for abstinence, employment, and improved personal and social functioning. It then reports treatment results back to the referring justice system agency. Clients who violate the conditions of their justice mandates (diversion, deferred sentencing, pretrial intervention, or probation), their TASC contracts, or their treatment agreements are typically returned to the justice system for continued processing or sanctions.

Within the context of this overview, the purposes of this chapter are as follows: (a) to review the social/historical context within which TASC emerged during the early 1970s; (b) to examine the theoretical, clinical, and pragmatic rationales for the establishment of TASC; (c) to consider TASC's initial operational structure; (d) to review the evaluations of TASC and how the program has changed; (e) to characterize the TASC of the 1980s and 1990s; and (f) to speculate on the future of TASC and its overall impact.

The Emergence of TASC

The 1960s and early 1970s were periods of rapid social change across the United States. They were times of civil rights and antiwar movements, the coming of age of the baby boom generation, new youth cultures and countercultures, and dramatic, raucous, and at times violent confrontations between the nation's minorities, youths, and young adults on the one hand and the older generations, political establishment, and traditional value structures on the other. The 1960s and early 1970s also were periods that reflected the complex interaction of the idealism of the Peace Corps, the rebellion of the inner cities, and the calls for altered states of consciousness through the use of a whole array of psychoactive drugs. And this "coming of age" in the United States occurred at the same time as major increases in all types of crime (see Gitlin, 1987; Inciardi, 1986; Viorst, 1979).

Reactions to the rebellion of youth, and to drug use and street crime, played a significant role in the election of Richard M. Nixon to the presidency in 1968. Appealing to the traditional values of middle America, to the great majority of Americans who did not riot, protest, or use drugs, Nixon successfully built a powerful and varied constituency. Moreover, it would appear from historical records that Nixon believed that the United States was in the midst of a drug revolution that threatened the very safety of its citizens (see Cronin, Cronin, & Milakovich, 1981; Epstein, 1977). Street crime was portrayed as rampant, and the president asked for and obtained major new powers to address the drug epidemic. In the opinion polls of the time, Americans were indicating that drug abuse and crime were among their major concerns.

The time was ripe for a presidential initiative, in part because prior to Nixon's entrance into the White House two new areas of consensus about drugs and crime problems had developed. First, during the 1960s, after many decades of indecision regarding how best to manage the drug-involved offender, an integration of criminal justice and mental health treatment perspectives began to emerge. Clinicians successfully argued that incarceration as a punishment for crime was not the solution for drug addiction. This came in the aftermath of *Robinson v. California,* which we have discussed in detail in Chapter 2. Although *Robinson* dealt primarily with the Eighth Amendment ban on cruel and unusual punishment, its lesser-known holding was that a state could establish a program of compulsory treatment for narcotics addiction.

Second, government officials as well as the public at large had come to view much of the criminal involvement of narcotics users as driven by economics—that is, the need to obtain money to buy drugs. It was believed that if drug dependency could be treated, then drug-related crime could be reduced, or even eliminated.

The Nixon administration's "war on drugs" built on these trends and thinking with the passage of the Comprehensive Drug Abuse Prevention and Control Act of 1970 (see Uelman & Haddox, 1989, sec. 3.2). More commonly known as the Controlled Substances Act, the legislation authorized, among other things, the diversion of drug-involved offenders from the criminal justice system into drug abuse treatment programs. Similar legislation was being passed in a number of state jurisdictions. At both the federal and state levels, the focus of diversion was on nonviolent first offenders, particularly those whose crimes were associated with heroin addiction.

By 1972, then, several statutory linkages had been created between the criminal justice and drug abuse treatment systems. It was at this point that the Treatment Alternatives to Street Crime program was created by President Nixon's Special Action Office for Drug Abuse Prevention. A national program designed to divert drug-involved offenders into appropriate community-based treatment programs, TASC was funded by the Law Enforcement Assistance Administration and the National Institute of Mental Health. The first programs became operational in Wilmington, Delaware, and Philadelphia, Pennsylvania, by the close of 1972 (Perlman & Jaszi, 1976, p. 2).

The Empirical and Theoretical Foundations of TASC

TASC evolved within the context of the prevailing theoretical, clinical, and empirical understandings of the relationship between drug use and crime. The program attempted to develop effective alternatives to the incarceration of drug-using criminal offenders. At a practical level, the implementation of TASC in 1972 was based on three fundamental assumptions:

1. "that in various parts of the United States, and particularly in major metropolitan areas, there were serious problems of drug abuse and addiction that both directly and indirectly affected significant portions of the population";
2. "that coupled with drug addiction was a cycle of crime, arrest, incarceration, release and more often than not, continued drug dependence that inhibited efforts to 'rehabilitate' the addict and safeguard the community"; and
3. "that the frequency of this contact between the addict and the criminal justice system provided viable opportunities for the introduction of treatment alternatives to street crime" (Law Enforcement Assistance Administration, 1973, p. 1).

As we have discussed at length in Chapter 1, one of the most consistent findings in social research during the decades preceding the early 1970s was the statistical relationship between criminal behavior and the use of illicit drugs. That relationship, furthermore, had been documented in research from a great variety of empirical and theoretical traditions, using a wide assortment of samples, indicators, and data collection techniques. High rates of illicit drug use and criminal behavior were repeatedly found within the same types of neighborhoods (Chein, 1966; Dai, 1937; Faris & Dunham, 1939), generally existing together as part of the same neighborhood milieu (see, for example, Agar, 1973; Inciardi, 1974). Other studies described the characteristics of users of illegal drugs, reporting that they committed numerous property crimes to obtain funds to purchase drugs (Inciardi & Chambers, 1972; O'Donnell, 1969). Examinations of arrestee populations frequently found that the majority engaged in illicit drug use (Eckerman, Bates, Raschal, & Poole, 1976; Ford, Hauser, & Jackson, 1975; McBride, 1976). It was even concluded that in many of the nation's major cities, the *majority* of property crimes were committed by heroin users (Inciardi, 1974; McBride, 1976; Research Triangle Institute, 1976).

Explanations of this empirical relationship between crime and drug use focused on three primary considerations: the legal system itself, the time sequence of addiction and criminal careers, and the economic demands of addiction. First, and as many observers and investigators noted, the possession of heroin, cocaine, marijuana, and a variety of other substances is illegal in and of itself. As such, some proportion of the drugs-crime relationship is accounted for on a de facto basis (see Lindesmith, 1965). The possession of illicit drugs and/or drug use-related paraphernalia, even in the absence of other criminal charges, indeed results in a significant proportion of drug users coming to the attention of the criminal justice system. However, survey data and analyses of arrest and court records demonstrate that many additional drug user contacts with criminal justice agencies result from crimes against property and persons.

Second, the question of causality in the drugs-crime connection is partly a matter of time sequence. By the mid-1970s it was clear that many drug users engaged in criminal activities before initiating expensive drug use (Voss & Stephens, 1973). However, studies also documented that drug abuse tends to both intensify and prolong criminal careers (Gandossy, Williams, Cohen, & Harwood, 1980; Inciardi, 1979; O'Donnell, 1969; Stephens & McBride, 1976). This suggested that significant proportions of the crime committed by drug users are the result of drug use.

Third, this causal direction has generally been explained in terms of the cost of drugs, the economic situation of the drug user, and the physiological and psychological demands of addiction. Most illegal drugs are expensive. In this regard, research during the early 1970s found that heroin users spent an average of some $35 per day for their drug of choice (Weppner & McBride, 1975). Because the great majority of heroin users had either low-paying jobs or no employment at all, property crime became their major means of drug use support.

Criminologists have devoted a significant amount of attention to the notion that criminal justice processing has unintended consequences that foster the very behaviors it is attempting to deter and prevent. These consequences are typically discussed in terms of *labeling* and *social learning* theories of crime. For the better part of the twentieth century, an assorted collection of researchers, theorists, and practitioners in the field of criminology have argued that arresting, processing, sentencing, incarcerating, and, hence, labeling individuals as "criminal" has major impacts on their self-concepts and consequent behaviors (Becker, 1963; Lemert, 1972). From this perspective, criminal justice processing causes individuals to regard themselves as criminals, which in turn motivates the individuals to engage in more frequent episodic criminal behavior. As applied to drug users, this perspective implies that those who might not otherwise have regarded themselves as criminals will do so as the direct result of being treated as criminals. Thus the criminal justice system itself can create additional links between drug use and crime.

Labeling an individual as criminal may also have broader sociological and economic consequences. As Schwartz and Skolnick (1963) note, being convicted of a felony or merely being accused of a serious crime can severely limit a person's occupational choices and access. With avenues to desirable legitimate social and economic roles blocked, the individual finds that the remaining rewarding roles are typically illegitimate ones. For drug users, the criminal label may enhance the social and economic isolation of individuals who, because of their status as "drug users" (and perhaps also as minority group members from inner-city neighborhoods), already have severe problems of societal integration.

A second perspective on the adverse consequences of criminal justice processing stresses the social learning effects of incarceration (for example, see Clemmer, 1950, 1958; Gibbons, 1965; Sutherland, 1937; Sykes, 1965). The basic notion is that prisoners, because of their associations and interaction patterns with other prisoners, learn a wide variety of criminal behaviors and attitudes. As a result, the ex-convict's repertoire of behaviors is typically even more focused on criminal roles than it was before the individual was incarcerated. Thus the social learning effects of incarceration, like the impact of criminal labeling, further link drug use and crime.

In addition to the behavioral costs of incarceration, its monetary expense is also problematic—ranging from $15,000 to $30,000 per inmate/year, depending on the institution and jurisdiction. During the years immediately prior to the implementation of TASC, court diversion was seen as one possible cost-effective alternative. TASC, in particular, was an outgrowth of all these considerations (American Bar Association Commission on Correctional Facilities Services, 1975).

The Early Years of TASC

The original TASC model of the early 1970s was structured around three goals: (a) eliminating (or at least reducing) the drug use and criminal behaviors of drug-involved offenders, (b) shifting drug-involved offenders from a system based on deterrence and punishment to one fostering treatment and rehabilitation, and (c) ameliorating the labeling and prison learning processes by diverting drug-involved offenders to community-based facilities before the application of criminal labels. In performing these functions, TASC focused on identifying drug users in the criminal justice system, gaining the cooperation of criminal justice agencies by promoting the efficacy of its approach, convincing drug-involved offenders of their need for diversion and treatment, creating links with community treatment systems, and transferring clients from criminal justice agencies to treatment programs (Law Enforcement Assistance Administration, 1973).

Because of its theoretical grounding, TASC's initial focus was the pretrial diversion of first offenders. The assumption was that, as first offenders had not yet been labeled criminals, treatment intervention had a better chance of success. It was also assumed that legislation at federal, state, and local levels would permit the diversion of drug-involved first offenders into treatment, and that such diversion would include the withholding of further criminal justice processing after arraignment, pending the outcome of treatment. The developers of TASC also presumed that criminal justice personnel *and clients* could be convinced of the value of TASC diversion. During the treatment process, TASC personnel would closely monitor treatment program compliance and client retention, with rapid communication to the court as to any problems. At completion of treatment, TASC clients' court cases would be dropped or dismissed. Thus there would be no adjudication or conviction, and hence no criminal labeling of first offenders and no incarceration in deviant learning environments.

Although these initial program ideas were based on recent social science theory, their implementation quickly became problematic. Diversion itself was not the issue. Legislators approved of the idea, the judiciary found it constitutionally acceptable, and prosecutors and judges were willing to try diversion with young, nonviolent offenders. The problem was labeling theory and the reality of heroin use. Experience quickly demonstrated that labeling theory had little applicability to the worlds of heroin use and street crime. The concept of a first offender/heroin user turned out to be an oxymoron: There was virtually no such thing. By the time drug users initiated heroin use, they had been heavy users of alcohol and other illegal drugs for quite some time, and had had extensive contacts with the criminal justice system. Moreover, research was demonstrating that criminal careers and criminal self-images were well developed long before the individuals involved had their initial contacts with the criminal justice system—not because of labeling, but because of the social learning processes that take place in drug-using subcultures.[1]

In addition, the courts often found that the educational histories, employment records, and unstable living arrangements of heroin users simply did not justify such nonjudicial processing as diversion. Prosecutors and judges were decidedly unwilling to divert heroin users with extensive criminal histories but few, if any, indicators of positive social functioning. And it is not surprising that TASC practitioners felt that labeling theory should have remained in the academic settings from which it came.

Another set of problems ensued from the fact that those drug users who *were* first offenders tended to be marijuana users. Treatment resources of the 1970s focused almost exclusively on heroin and heroin/polydrug users. Moreover, arrested marijuana users generally refused to participate in diversion programs. In their judgment (and in that of their attorneys), they were better off taking their chances with the criminal justice system (e.g., plea-bargaining for probation) rather than agreeing to a 6-, 12-, or 18-month treatment program.

Within a short time after its initiation, TASC broadened its definition of appropriate clients from first offenders to *all* drug-involved offenders the courts would divert, sentence, or otherwise probate to treatment. By 1977, TASC clients were equally divided between pretrial diversion and posttrial sentencing (System Sciences, 1979).

Early Appraisals of TASC

By the late 1970s, TASC had been in operation in a sufficient number of jurisdictions and for a long enough period to warrant an evaluation of its impact. More specifically, evaluation was deemed appropriate in such areas as due process issues in TASC diversion, the ability of TASC to identify drug-involved offenders, TASC's ability to make the link between the criminal justice and treatment systems, the acceptance of TASC by treatment programs, and treatment success of TASC clients.

Due Process Issues in TASC Diversion

Both the judiciary and representatives of the legal profession had been active in the early discussions of the drugs-crime connection and the inadequacy of the existing system in reducing drug-related crime. Attorneys and judges were among the most enthusiastic supporters of TASC, both for philosophical reasons and because of the pragmatic problems presented by a court system bogged down by opiate-using offenders. In 1976, however, the American Bar Association addressed the constitutionality of criminal justice diversion (see Perlman & Jaszi, 1976), touching on such matters as self-incrimination, search and seizure, equal protection, confidentiality of records, and treatment termination.

Self-Incrimination and Unreasonable Search and Seizure

In the early days of TASC, the criteria for diversion into treatment involved the documentation of drug use in general and opiate use in particular. This documentation involved physical examinations, self-reports, and/or urinalysis results. In most jurisdictions, client screening procedures tended to be broad, sometimes uniformly applied to *all* arrestees. Although the purpose of such information gathering was based on a rehabilitative ideal, its compulsory nature represented infringements of defendants' rights. At issue were the Fourth Amendment's proscription against illegal search and seizure and the Fifth Amendment's protection against self-incrimination. Thus some critics felt that TASC had arguable constitutional grounding.

Although the U.S. Supreme Court had ruled in *Robinson v. California* that being a narcotic addict was a "status" not punishable under the law, documentation of drug use implied the possession of illegal substances (and perhaps quantities sufficient to imply intent to sell). Further, there were many TASC-eligible arrestees who, for one reason or another, preferred prosecution over diversion. And there were many more who were ineligible for diversion. In all of these instances, extensive data were being collected that documented drug use and perhaps other activities that carried the potential for self-incrimination.

The issue of urine testing was (and continues to be) subject to serious debate. At the inception of TASC, urine was typically viewed as abandoned property—something that was routinely expelled and abandoned in all known cultures. The only U.S. Supreme Court decision analogous at the time to routine urine sampling was *Schmerber v. California,* decided in 1966. In *Schmerber,* which involved a forced blood-alcohol test of a nonconsenting motorist, the Court ruled that the puncture of the human body to obtain blood represented illegal search and seizure, in violation of the Fourth Amendment. The Court ruled, however, that such a test would be permissible in the presence of probable cause. *Schmerber* has been applied to urine in the sense that the state has the right to obtain blood, breath, *and urine* as part of its regulatory function.

With regard to diversion and TASC, the function of urine collection and analysis was considered *not* for the purposes of prosecution, conviction, and sentencing, but for the purpose of advising the judge and other court officers in the best interests of the defendant and the public. Although the 1975 American Bar Association report recognized the basis of this argument for urinalysis and diversion, it nevertheless noted that the constitutional basis of state-compelled urine provisions rested on uncertain assumptions. The issues of compelling urine samples, who may compel them, and the purposes for which they may be used are still debated and unresolved. However, TASC procedures view urine screening as involving non-constitutionally protected property. For the time being, the courts continue to view such coerced urine sampling as part of the regulatory purposes of government, and as an instrument of rehabilitation.

TASC Eligibility Requirements and Equal Protection

As noted above, TASC procedures included specific eligibility criteria that restricted client selection. These criteria were determined by TASC, individual court systems, and treatment programs. Although selection procedures represented barriers to treatment for some defendants, TASC appeared to be operating on firm constitutional ground.

Prior to the establishment of TASC, the federal government had already restricted offender access to treatment. The Narcotic Addict Rehabilitation Act (NARA) of 1966 specifically excluded from sentencing to treatment those offenders with two or more prior felony convictions. This provision was tested in *Marshall v. United States,* decided by the Supreme Court in 1974, and became the constitutional basis for NARA, TASC, and similar programs. In *Marshall,* the Court held by a 6 to 3 vote that the NARA selection criteria were based on a rational relationship argument and did not violate the equal protection clause of the Fourteenth Amendment. The majority decision focused on the reasoning that those convicted of two or more felonies were likely older, more hardened offenders with longer addiction careers and therefore more difficult to treat. It seemed reasonable to the Court that the government could restrict treatment opportunities to those offenders it had reason to believe would be most amenable to treatment—those who were earlier in their drug careers and not as entrenched in the drugs-crime lifestyle.

Confidentiality of Treatment Records

Drug abuse treatment involves the collection of data on incriminating activities, such as drug sales, prostitution, and crimes against persons and property. However, the Comprehensive Drug Abuse Prevention and Control Act of 1970 (42 U.S.C., Sec. 242[a] [1970], 21 U.S.C., Sec. 872[c] [1970]) and Section 408 of the Federal Drug Abuse Office and Treatment Act of 1972 (21 U.S.C., Sec. 1175 [1972]) protect research data and therapeutic records in a variety of ways. It had been the belief of Congress that passage of the 1970 and 1972 legislation would be in the public interest, in that the new protections might encourage research and participation in treatment.

The extent to which treatment records, including urinalysis results, are protected from courts and law enforcement remains unclear. However, it would appear from the lack of court challenges by criminal justice agencies that *all* treatment data on diverted clients are protected. This situation applied to criminal justice clients as well, and likely played a major role in the acceptance of TASC by potential clients and drug treatment programs alike.[2]

Treatment Termination

The termination from treatment of TASC-diverted clients involved a number of considerations. Generally, the client was diverted to treatment while prosecution was held in abeyance, or as a condition of probation. Treatment termination thus had major criminal justice implications.

The legal issues surrounding termination focus on three areas: (a) legally permissible grounds for termination, (b) procedures required in terminating a person's diversion or probation program, and (c) legally permissible results of termination. With regard to the first two concerns, TASC has maintained that a judge's decision to send a drug-involved offender into treatment (through diversion or probation) represents the court's acceptance of the reasonable standards and procedures of the treatment program, including the conditions under which the program would terminate a client. The third issue, results of termination, is likewise relatively unproblematic. For pretrial diversion cases, termination from treatment represents neither the commission of a crime nor an admission of guilt on the original charge. Rather, it initiates a resumption of the original judicial proceedings (with all of the associated due process safeguards guaranteed by the Bill of Rights) that had been interrupted by the diversion to treatment.

In the case of diversion as a condition of probation, treatment termination did not represent an automatic revocation. Rather, the revocation process was controlled by a series of due process safeguards announced by the U.S. Supreme Court in *Mempa v. Rhay, Morrissey v. Brewer,* and *Gagnon v. Scarpelli.*[3]

Identification of Drug Users

One of the major purposes of TASC was (and remains) the identification of drug-involved offenders. At its inception, and as already noted, TASC programs generally used mass urine screening procedures to identify potential clients. However, in addition to the due process questions that mass screening raised, the approach was both labor-intensive and costly. Subsequent comparisons of urinalysis results with self-report data on drug use found considerable correspondence between the two.[4] Thus, within a few years after the initiation of TASC, programs had begun to move away from mass urine screening. In addition, as TASC expanded to include more serious offenders and probationers, the need for urine screening became less compelling. Data sources evolved to include client self-reports (and some urinalysis summaries) augmented by information from police and prosecutors and presentence investigation reports when ordered by a judge.

The TASC evaluation conducted in 1976 concluded that programs had been successful in identifying a large number of offenders qualified for TASC services, and that self-reports, urinalysis, and referrals from judges and attorneys appeared to generate a large client flow (Toborg, Levin, Milkman, & Center, 1976). The evaluators noted, however, that it was difficult to determine the effectiveness of TASC in identifying all eligible clients, or how selection processes were operating. Yet, overall, it was clear that TASC had been successful in identifying those drug-involved offenders in need of services and in delivering them to drug treatment programs. It was also evident that this success was based on TASC's own screening techniques as well as the strong cooperation of the judiciary and other officers of the court (Collins, Hubbard, Raschal, Cavanaugh, & Craddock, 1982b; System Sciences, 1979; Toborg et al., 1976).

The client selection issue noted by the 1976 TASC evaluation (Toborg et al., 1976) raises interesting questions as to the proportion of the eligible population TASC selects and who agrees to participate in TASC. Both issues appear to have become more problematic over time. For several decades, the state and local courts have been somewhat overwhelmed by the sheer number of cases they must handle. The speedy trial requirement of the Sixth Amendment places additional strains on local systems, and the federal judiciary closely monitors crowding problems in prisons and jails. As a result, many cases never come to trial, pretrial release procedures have become less rigid, jail and prison sentences have become shorter, and technical violations of the conditions of probation and parole less often result in incarceration. And, it is important to note, judges are less likely to incarcerate drug-involved offenders for failure to participate in a treatment program.

Experienced offenders are well aware of these contingencies, including the actual odds against their "doing time." During the late 1970s, a Miami, Florida, study comparing the characteristics of TASC clients with those of TASC eligibles who declined participation offered some interesting findings. A total of 2,529 drug-involved felony arrestees were randomly sampled from Miami's central booking facility. Self-reports and urinalysis were used to determine drug use. All were asked to volunteer for TASC, but less than 20% were willing. Those who chose TASC diversion were more likely to be black, 25 years of age or older, exclusively opiate using, high school dropouts, and unemployed (McBride & Bennett, 1978). These data suggest that TASC may be attracting only the more difficult cases, individuals who see themselves as the most likely to be convicted and sentenced to incarceration. As such, they view TASC as an alternative to incarceration. By contrast, arrestees who were younger, less criminally involved, and with jobs and high school diplomas may well have concluded that they were better off dealing with the courts directly, that they would probably face sentences less severe than diversion to treatment. And although the Miami data are limited to but one location, they illustrate a dimension of possible offender responses to TASC.

Linking the Justice and Treatment Systems

Prior to TASC, there were few effective links between the criminal justice process and drug abuse treatment. During those years, there were a scattering of criminal justice clients in prisons, and in probation/parole settings, who had access to drug abuse treatment. The great majority of these, furthermore, were narcotics addicts in New York and California.

Specific programs for the treatment of drug abusers in prison settings during the 1960s through the early 1970s were as diversified as programs in the free community. They included group therapy (Dwyer, 1971; Rosenthal & Shimberg, 1958), chemical detoxification (Dole, 1972), therapeutic communities (Farkas, Petersen, & Barr, 1970; Petersen, Yarvis, & Farkas, 1969), ex-addict counseling (Farkas et al., 1970), and methadone maintenance (Dole et al., 1969). Despite a considerable body of descriptive and philosophical writing on these early prison-based approaches, it would appear from the literature that few evaluations were conducted. Moreover, including the federal NARA effort, effective linkages between treatment and justice were for the most part absent. Rather, the overwhelming majority of prison-based interventions operated independent of local treatment delivery systems. As a result, most failed to provide patient aftercare following release to the community (Petersen, 1974).

The literature suggests that during the 20-year period beginning in the early 1950s, there were a number of programs involving the community-based treatment of probationers and parolees (Adams & McArthur, 1969; Bailey, 1956; Brill & Lieberman, 1970; Diskind & Klonsky, 1964a, 1964b; Joseph & Dole, 1970). A review of these studies suggests that although large numbers of probationers and parolees received treatment in local treatment programs, formalized linkages between treatment and probation/parole agencies were absent. Typically, treatment referrals and admissions were accomplished through friendships and special arrangements orchestrated by individual probation/parole officers with specific staff members in selected treatment programs. As such, linkages were made through personal contacts. When these officers transferred to other jobs, referral arrangements evaporated.

By contrast, the civil commitment experiences in California and New York during the 1960s reflected highly structured criminal justice-treatment linkages, but for the most part these operated independent of existing community-based treatment programs. The California Civil Addict Program (CAP), initiated in 1961, had its own inpatient and outpatient facilities (McGlothlin, Anglin, & Wilson, 1977). As such, the linkage was between the justice system and the civil commitment bureaucracy. A similar situation existed with New York State's Narcotic Addiction Control Commission (NACC). In addition to its own institutional and aftercare facilities, large caseloads forced NACC to purchase treatment beds from independent community-based programs. As noted in Chapter 2, however, NACC was so poorly organized and operated that it is difficult now to determine whether or not the linkages were effective (Inciardi, 1988). Moreover, whatever linkages existed were between the civil commitment bureaucracy and treatment programs, and thus bypassed the criminal justice system.

By the second half of the 1970s, on the other hand, it was clear that TASC had indeed bridged criminal justice agencies with local drug abuse treatment systems. The best evidence of this success is reflected in how TASC altered the client characteristics of treatment program populations. Although there are drug users with criminal records in virtually every treatment program, TASC significantly expanded their proportions. Three studies, one in Charlotte, North Carolina, a second in Miami, and the national Treatment Outcome Prospective Study (TOPS) indicate this impact.

In both Miami and Charlotte, TASC significantly increased the number of clients entering treatment. Furthermore, there were increases in the proportions of clients with arrest histories (McBride & Bennett, 1978). Data from TOPS, a large-scale effort funded by the National Institute on Drug Abuse, showed that in comparison to non-TASC clients, TASC clients were likely to have used illegal drugs more frequently and to have acquired larger proportions of their income from illegal sources (Collins et al., 1982b).

Treatment Outcomes of TASC Clients

Treatment impacts and outcomes must be considered in a relative sense. If success in treatment is defined to include permanent and total abstinence from drug abuse and criminal activity, uninterrupted full-time employment, and stable residence and family situations, then treatment "successes" would be rare indeed. By contrast, researchers and clinicians look not for "success" or "failure," but *progress in treatment* and *treatment outcomes* as more realistic indicators of treatment impacts. Measures of progress and positive outcomes include such indicators as length of stay in treatment, reduced drug use, lower rates of recidivism, longer periods of abstinence, increased employability, and greater economic independence.

Assessing TASC's impacts on client outcomes is not always possible, because impacts occur in great part as the result of the treatment program's therapeutic efforts. TASC participation in the treatment process involves influencing clients to enter and remain in treatment. Thus a direct measure of TASC impact would involve a comparison of length of stay in treatment for TASC clients and length of stay for non-TASC clients. Because length of stay has been demonstrated to be linked directly to treatment outcome, indicators of TASC monitoring would include greater reductions in drug use and criminality and higher rates of employment among TASC versus non-TASC clients.

The early national evaluations of TASC did not examine client outcomes from these perspectives (see System Sciences, 1979; Toborg et al., 1976). TOPS reports on 1979 and 1980 cohorts of drug users entering treatment, however, provided data on TASC versus non-TASC clients (Collins & Allison, 1983; Collins, Hubbard, Raschal, Cavanaugh, & Craddock, 1982a, 1982b). Clients who were referred to TOPS programs through a TASC program differed systematically from other TOPS clients on a variety of dimensions. TASC-referred clients were more likely to be male, young, and nonwhite. There were also differences in the pretreatment drug use patterns and in other characteristics of TASC and non-TASC clients. TASC clients were more likely to report recent arrest and incarceration and to report illegal sources of income. Thus the TOPS data supported the interpretation that appropriate drug-abusing offenders were being referred to drug treatment by TASC.

An analysis of treatment retention and treatment outcomes indicated that TASC clients remained in treatment longer than non-TASC clients and did at least as well as non-TASC clients on the outcome measures of drug use, depressive symptoms, illegal activity, and employment while in treatment. The TOPS reports also demonstrated that criminal justice involvement per se influenced outcome: Clients who were involved with the criminal justice system stayed in treatment longer than those who were not. In addition, TASC-referred clients remained in treatment longer than did non-TASC criminal justice clients (Hubbard, Collins, Raschal, & Cavanaugh, 1988).

Cost-Benefit Considerations

A major objective of the TASC initiative was to reduce the costs of dealing with drug-involved offenders. The argument was that it would be more cost-effective to treat drug users than to incarcerate them. The results of the national evaluation of TASC at the close of the 1970s suggested that the TASC effort had indeed been a cost-effective initiative (System Sciences, 1979). Among the programs studied in this evaluation, it was determined that the cost of processing a TASC client was $637. In addition, annual treatment costs varied from $2,662 for outpatient programs to $6,212 for residential programs. Thus it was estimated that the maximum cost for identifying, referring, monitoring, and treating a TASC client was no more than $7,000 annually (in late 1970s dollars).

The estimate for the court processing of a drug-involved offender (with a trial by judge or jury and a not-guilty verdict) was a maximum of $5,000, suggesting that TASC could be a more costly process in some instances. However, for convictions resulting in incarceration, costs quickly escalated to more than $14,000 per year. In addition, it was argued that there were other significant cost-benefits to TASC. As noted earlier in the TOPS data, TASC clients in treatment typically reduced their drug intake, and hence their associated criminal activity. The national evaluation study estimated that for clients with $50-a-day habits, 6 months in TASC had a potential savings of some $51,000 (based on the proportion of drug funds coming from crime and the fencing of stolen property at only a fraction of its actual market value).

In summary, the preliminary evaluations during the 1970s suggested that TASC had been quite successful in gaining acceptance. Local courts were being overwhelmed by the sheer number of cases and by the increasing numbers of opiate-using offenders. Once TASC broadened its role beyond first offenders to include more serious offenders and probations, judges and legislators extended their support. Furthermore, TASC seemed to have stable constitutional footing.

The Current Structure of TASC

To a very great extent, the roots of TASC can be traced not only to the LEAA, but also to the President's Commission on Law Enforcement and Administration of Justice and the "war on crime" of the late 1960s and early 1970s. TASC was but one among many initiatives. Well before the 1980s had begun, however, it was all too clear that the national war on crime had failed. The great LEAA experiment had not uncovered the secret to solving the crime problem. What it did show, however, was what did not work in preventing crime: saturation patrolling, quicker police response times, advanced technology, and college education for law enforcement personnel. LEAA studies also served to deflate optimistic notions about the rehabilitation of offenders, preventive detention, parole, and the death penalty as a deterrent to homicide (see Cronin et al., 1981). From its inception in 1969 through 1980, LEAA appropriations totaled almost $8 billion.

On April 15, 1982, LEAA was terminated; the reasons were numerous. During its formative years, LEAA had struggled to reduce crime and to respond to changing congressional priorities while managing a rapidly expanding budget. But by the mid-1970s, as the crime rate kept accelerating and the criticisms of LEAA continued unabated, inflation-conscious presidents began submitting reduced budget requests for the agency. The major criticisms included mismanagement in grant programs, inefficiency and ineffectiveness, inconsistent objectives, and lack of standards and criteria for evaluating program effectiveness. With inflation reaching new heights at the beginning of the 1980s, LEAA was given only minimal funding for 1981. And finally, there was the "new federalism"—that emergent political consensus that reduced federal involvement in direct services to local communities. With the demise of LEAA in 1982, federal funding was completely withdrawn from TASC. At the time, TASC were operating at 130 sites in 39 different states and Puerto Rico (U.S. Department of Justice, 1988, p. 5).

Despite the demise of LEAA, TASC has not only endured, but has done so rather well. Immediately after the withdrawal of federal funding, some 100 programs in 18 jurisdictions were able to secure local support. The Justice Assistance Act of 1984 revived federal endorsement and some fiscal support for TASC. This legislation authorized a criminal justice block grant program to encourage local and state government support of programs deemed highly likely to improve the efficiency and effectiveness of the criminal justice system and to address the problems of drug-related crime and the drug-involved offender.

As TASC moved through the 1980s, changes in attitudes and policies at the national level tended to have impacts. The election of Ronald Reagan to the presidency of the United States ushered in a new "war on drugs" characterized by both "supply reduction" and "demand reduction" strategies. Supply reduction focused on *interdiction* (the interception of vessels and aircraft attempting to smuggle illegal drugs into the United States), foreign assistance initiatives, and law enforcement and other operations designed to reduce the supply of drugs available to consumers. Demand reduction strategies focused on prevention, education, and treatment. TASC was viewed in many jurisdictions as a respected demand reduction strategy already linked to the justice system. As a result, TASC continued to prosper through the 1980s and into the 1990s.

Postscript

The TASC experience has been a positive one. TASC has been demonstrated to be highly productive in (a) identifying populations of drug-involved offenders in great need of treatment, (b) assessing the nature and extent of their drug use patterns and specific treatment needs, (c) effectively referring drug-involved offenders to treatment, (d) serving as a link between the criminal justice and treatment systems, and (e) providing constructive client identification and monitoring services for the courts, probation, and other segments of the criminal justice system. Perhaps most important, evaluation data indicate that TASC-referred clients remain longer in treatment than non-TASC clients and, as a result, have better posttreatment success.

As the nation's attempts at drug control move through the 1990s, there are some very good reasons for expanding TASC. First, there is the changing relationship between drug use and crime. Whereas the drug-involved offender in the early days of TASC was a primary heroin user with a long history of property offenses, much of the drug-related crime of the 1990s is far more violent (McBride & Swartz, 1990). Moreover, Drug Use Forecasting data document that instead of there being a statistical relationship between drugs and crime, it would appear that there is a saturation of drugs in offender populations.

Research conducted during the 1980s on the specific effects of drug use on patterns of criminal behavior suggests that TASC can play a significant role in reducing drug-related street crime. In a series of excellent research analyses, John C. Ball of the Addiction Research Center and David N. Nurco of the University of Maryland have demonstrated that during their drug-*free* days, members of drug subcultures are far less likely to commit crimes than during their drug-*using* days (Ball, Shaffer, & Nurco, 1983; Nurco, Ball, Shaffer, & Hanlon, 1985). TASC has been effective in identifying, assessing, referring, and monitoring members of such populations.

Second, the 1980s and 1990s wars on drugs and citizen demands for more drug arrests and convictions have tended to exacerbate the already crowded conditions in court settings throughout the country. The wider use of TASC as a mechanism of pretrial diversion or in conjunction with probation could serve to alleviate some of this crowding.

Third, there is a link between drug use and the spread of AIDS (acquired immune deficiency syndrome). The ready acquisition and transmission of HIV (human immunodeficiency virus—the virus that causes AIDS) among injection drug users is the result of the sharing of injection equipment, combined with the presence of "cofactors" that may include behavioral practices or microbiological agents that facilitate the transmission of HIV. For heroin, cocaine, and amphetamine users who inject their drugs, the blood transmission of HIV may occur as a result of using or sharing contaminated drug injection paraphernalia. Prior to injection, the user's drug of choice must be made into a solution; usually it is dissolved in tap water and heated in a "cooker"—typically a bottle cap or spoon. Because cookers, which are rarely cleaned properly, are often shared by injection drug users, they represent potential reservoirs for HIV.

The injection process poses even greater contamination risks. "Booting" is a risk/cofactor of considerable significance, because the practice increases the amount of residual blood left in drug paraphernalia. Booting involves the aspiration of venous blood back into a syringe for the purpose of mixing the drug with blood, while the needle remains inserted in the vein. The mixed blood-and-drug solution is then injected back into the vein. Most injection drug users believe that this "premixing" enhances a drug's effects. Because users often share needles and syringes, particularly if they are administering the drugs in "shooting galleries"—places where users gather to take drugs—booting increases the probability that traces of HIV from an infected user will remain in a syringe to be passed on to the next user. Finally, genital sores and infections from other viruses have also been found to be cofactors (Quinn et al., 1988), and because of their lifestyles, injection drug users are rather well known as a population that hosts a wide spectrum of microorganisms (Des Jarlais et al., 1987; Geelhoed, 1984; Young, 1973).

An additional risk factor in the AIDS-IV drug connection is prostitution, including the exchange of sex for drugs—particularly among crack-dependent men and women. There is an extensive body of literature offering a strong empirical basis for the notion that prostitution is a major means of economic support for drug-using women (Goldstein, 1979; Inciardi, 1986; James, 1976; Rosenbaum, 1981). As such, the drug-using prostitute is at high risk not only for contracting HIV, but for transmitting it as well (Castro et al., 1988; Chaisson, Moss, Onishi, Osmond, & Carlson, 1987; Newmeyer, 1987). Furthermore, the transmission of HIV has increased significantly as a result of the trading of sex for crack cocaine (Inciardi, Lockwood, & Pottieger, 1993; Ratner, 1993).

Drug users, in addition to being the group at second-highest risk for HIV and AIDS, also represent a population that appears to be difficult to reach with routine AIDS prevention messages. Most drug users probably are aware of the potential for HIV acquisition and transmission from infected paraphernalia and "unsafe" sex, but they are accustomed to risking death (through overdose or the violence-prone nature of the illegal drug marketplace) and disease (hepatitis and other infections) on a daily basis, and such risks generally fail to eliminate their drug-taking behaviors. Thus, for drug users, warnings that needle sharing or unsafe sex may facilitate an infection that could cause death perhaps 5 or more years down the road have little meaning. Given that, an appropriate risk reduction strategy for this population would be drug abuse treatment, as facilitated through TASC programming.

TASC and Parole

Given the demands in recent years for more and longer prison sentences for convicted felons, American prison systems are faced with a situation of massive overcrowding. Considering that perhaps half or more of all prison inmates are incarcerated as a result of drug use, an ideal area for TASC expansion is the parole setting.

Upon community re-entry, most parolees are confronted with a variety of obstacles. There are any number of environmental, familial, social, and peer group pressures that may contribute to violation of the conditions of parole and/or crime commission. These pressures tend to be especially acute for those with histories of drug involvement. Intervention into the drug-abusing lifestyle is perhaps the most difficult challenge faced by either parole officers/agents or treatment practitioners. Moreover, there are systemic communication problems, such as communication lapses between treatment providers and parole authorities, that exacerbate these difficulties.

Given this pivotal period for parolees with histories of drug involvement, an effective aftercare support system designed to foster alternate lifestyles and behaviors is crucial. Yet, in the majority of jurisdictions, prison crowding and excessively large parole caseloads have hindered the efficacy of both preparole and aftercare supervision services. The establishment of coordinated programming by parole and TASC can assist in reducing the factors that hinder success.

The ideal parole-TASC venture would be a joint effort between a jurisdiction's department of correction, parole authority, and the single state agency that oversees the provision of drug abuse treatment services. Although such a venture may appear to be fraught with potential for overlap and the problems of dual supervision, TASC can be structured to both enhance and complement parole supervision in a number of ways.

First, in the area of *preparole screening*, TASC assists the institutional correctional system in its role as a specialist in the identification and assessment of drug-involved offenders. Preparole screenings conducted through TASC tend to provide comprehensive background data on drug abuse and related behaviors that can serve as a basis for informed release decisions. For the paroling authority and its community supervision staff, this information represents a more thorough appraisal than would otherwise be available of the severity of the offender's drug problem and his or her potential risk to the community.

Second, in the area of *service delivery*, TASC offers advantages for both corrections and parole. TASC case managers specialize in developing and implementing aftercare plans for drug-involved offenders. In addition to drug abuse treatment, TASC provides urine monitoring, employment advocacy, client referral to other segments of the local human service delivery network, and follow-up. As such, treatment and support services can be offered within a "clinical" rather than a "correctional" setting. The parole authority benefits in that its primary responsibility of *supervision* is neither limited nor compromised by a parolee's treatment needs.

Third, in the area of *clinical efficacy,* the literature suggests that TASC represents an effective adjunct to parole. In this regard, a variety of research efforts have documented that (a) the key variable most related to successful outcome in drug treatment is *length of stay in treatment,* and (b) clients coerced into treatment tend to stay longer than those admitted voluntarily (Hubbard et al., 1989; Leukefeld & Tims, 1988). The TASC model is a variety of coerced treatment and, as noted earlier, has been proven effective in retaining clients in treatment.

Fourth, in the area of *alleviating prison crowding,* TASC can assist in two ways. TASC recommendations for treatment can ensure that scarce treatment slots will be allocated to those drug users most in need of, and likely to be responsive to, treatment. Accurate assessment of client needs increases the chances of success in treatment and reduces the chances of relapse and future criminal behavior, arrest, and incarceration. Further, TASC aids the parolee in successfully completing his or her term of supervision. Periodic urine tests, site visits, and case conferences tend to be useful deterrents that foster program compliance.

TASC and Work Release

A related consideration is the matter of TASC programming within the context of work release. Temporary release from prison and partial incarceration in transitional facilities and halfway houses have a notable history in American corrections. Justification of such forms of release draws upon a variety of theoretical and empirical traditions that emphasize the importance of individuals' maintaining significant, nondeviant roles outside the prison community (McBride & Swartz, 1990). Participation in a temporary release or halfway house program is considered to facilitate the individual's reintegration into the social and economic structures of the free community, thereby reducing his or her probability of recidivism. In addition, when the release also involves *work,* the offender is afforded opportunities to make restitution, pay fines, support dependents, obtain job training and experience, and perhaps make contacts for permanent employment upon eventual release from custody.

It would appear that TASC programming as an aspect of a structured work release program would be an ideal approach for prevention/intervention efforts for drug-involved offenders. In addition to the benefits of TASC discussed earlier in this chapter, an even greater potential exists within the context of TASC *as a condition of work release*. We have noted the clinical efficacy of compulsory or coerced treatment. Compulsory treatment for drug abuse has been legally possible in the United States for almost three decades, and for almost as long, researchers have been examining its relative effectiveness.

Although the benefits of coerced/compulsory treatment accrue within the context of any TASC arrangement, they would be intensified in a structured work release setting because of the close supervision associated with halfway houses and temporary release centers.

The Challenges and Future of TASC

In the late 1990s, TASC continues to evolve (or, more accurately, adapt) as drug control strategies accommodate to fluctuating public opinion and political forces. In doing so, TASC faces a number of challenges to its operational structure, activities, and goals, as well as to its very existence. The first of these stresses a complex of social and operational factors, and the second relates to the emergence of the new drug courts.

Although research has conclusively documented that "treatment works," the effectiveness of treatment is measured in small increments and typically requires a significant period of time. Childhood developmental experiences, family background, neighborhood "subcultures," education, self-esteem, and other individual characteristics have proven to be powerful influences on treatment progress and outcomes. Yet given the severe budget constraints faced by TASC as well as the treatment programs to which TASC refers clients, it is usually difficult (and sometimes impossible) to obtain the funds necessary to assess or serve clients' needs. It is often not understood that even if TASC offers the best possible assessment, the most appropriate treatment placement, and vigilant monitoring services, durable aspects of clients' backgrounds will have major influences on treatment outcomes. For example, it is not realistic to expect TASC activities to cause dramatic changes in an individual who has used crack for the past 10 years, who left school after the ninth grade, and whose primary source of income has always been illegal activities. TASC's roles involve assessment, referral, and monitoring, but its perceived effectiveness is ultimately dependent on the quality of the treatment programs to which it sends its clients. In short, the services offered by the highest-quality TASC program would be severely compromised by a treatment center characterized by only minimal clinical efficiency.

The etiology of drug abuse is both complex and inextricably linked to a host of developmental, interpersonal, environmental, economic, and cultural experiences. Although treatment can reasonably be expected to deal with some of these variables, it is impossible for treatment to affect the economic conditions that could provide viable opportunities for recovering addicts to change the sociocultural milieu to which they will return or to change institutional and cultural racism. These considerations represent serious limitations on the effectiveness of all human services programs.

As a final point here, judges and the judicial system appear to support TASC because they perceive it to be an extension of their offices—as providing additional monitoring (in the form of urinalysis) or staff that help them deal with their overloaded calendars and work schedules. But it must be remembered that, in general, judges represent the last stronghold of feudalism in the United States, and judges recognize that, organizationally, TASC programs do not report to them. This often has been the source of considerable frustration among judges intent on dealing with the extraordinary number of drug abusers coming before them. With TASC, they must work through a standard protocol for requesting and receiving reports, and they cannot officially (or even unofficially) easily direct TASC staff. Thus judges often see TASC as a "third party"—another layer between the judge and the services he or she has decided the drug-involved offender "needs." This dynamic has been critical in the judicial grassroots movement to establish drug courts. New rules for interaction and the program's degree of integration with these new courts will be crucial to TASC's effectiveness and continued existence.

Notes

1. For data supportive of these assertions, see Inciardi and Chambers (1972), Research Triangle Institute (1976), Inciardi (1979), Nurco et al. (1985), and Inciardi and Pottieger (1986).

2. Neither the Comprehensive Drug Abuse Prevention and Control Act of 1970 nor Section 408 of the Federal Drug Abuse Office and Treatment Act of 1972 are perfect protections. The 1970 act is restricted in coverage to "persons engaged in research." The 1972 act makes certain disclosures of addiction treatment data a

criminal offense, but contains a mechanism by which the disclosure of records can be compelled "for good cause." This provision was tested, however, in *People v. Newman,* decided by the New York State Court of Appeals in 1973, in which the court held that the director of a New York City methadone program could not be compelled to provide police with patient records.

3. In *Mempa v. Rhay* (1967), the Court's ruling required that counsel be provided at those probation revocation proceedings involving deferred sentencing, and excluded those cases when the probationer was sentenced at the time of trial. Other courts have extended the *Mempa* ruling to all revocation proceedings. *Morrissey v. Brewer* was decided by the U.S. Supreme Court in 1972. Although this case related to parole revocation hearings, it ultimately had significance for probation clients. The Court held that a parolee facing revocation is entitled to both a preliminary hearing to determine whether he or she actually violated parole and a final hearing to consider not only the facts in question but, if there was a violation, what to do about it. In *Gagnon v. Scarpelli* (1973), the Court held that a probationer, like a parolee, is entitled to the due process protections extended in *Morrissey v. Brewer*.

4. These studies were conducted in Denver, Philadelphia, and Cleveland during 1973 and 1974. See Toborg et al. (1976, pp. 3-4).

```
┌─────────────────────────────────┐
│  ╔═══════════════════════════╗  │
│  ║                           ║  │
│  ║      4. Drug Courts       ║  │
│  ║           and             ║  │
│  ║      Drug Treatment       ║  │
│  ║                           ║  │
│  ╚═══════════════════════════╝  │
└─────────────────────────────────┘
```

All human behavior occurs within sociotemporal contexts, and a full understanding of social phenomena requires knowledge of the zeitgeist—the general intellectual, moral, and cultural climate of the time—in which that behavior occurs. In the context of this discussion, the phenomenon is something called *drug courts,* which, narrowly considered, might be viewed as a relatively simple judicial innovation in case processing. Drug courts, or *court-enforced drug treatment programs* (the preferred term for the model receiving the most attention), can be best understood through a review of their initiation and development against the background of government antidrug policy and reactions to it on the part of the criminal justice system and other segments of society over the past decade.

The Sociopolitical Context

During much of the 1980s, there was immense frustration as both informed observers and the general public concluded that the nation's "war on drugs" was being lost. Despite the passage of the Anti-Drug Abuse Act of 1986, which allocated massive federal funding for drug control, impatience and cynicism were being expressed regarding the political response, particularly at the federal level, to the crack cocaine epidemic (Cowan, 1986; Press, 1986). Neither military leaders ("Defense Demurs," 1986) nor Congress (Shannon, 1989) embraced new federal plans to expand the military's role in the war on drugs. The avalanche of new federal and state legislation in response to media-fanned public and lawmakers' concerns about illicit drug use was just beginning to be examined critically (Kreiter, 1987).[1]

Many welcomed the passage of the Anti-Drug Abuse Act, but federal efforts were far from being universally praised; critics declared that the response to the spread of crack use had been too slow (Salholz, 1989), that the drug war was already lost (Buckley, 1989), or that it was "the wrong drug war" ("Off to War," 1989; "The Wrong Drug War," 1989). Some critics questioned the "drug war-national security" connection (Morley & Byrne, 1989); others questioned whether turf wars among the myriad entities (11 cabinet departments and 32 federal and 5 independent agencies) with some responsibility for drug control could be curtailed (Waldman, 1989), even by the new "drug czar," Dr. William Bennett (Corn, Gravley, & Morley, 1989; Morganthau & Miller, 1989). Bennett, head of the newly created Office of National Drug Control Policy, was administratively handicapped by having less authority (below cabinet level) than was intended by the members of Congress who advocated establishment of the position (McLaughlin, 1989). His effectiveness was also seen by some critics as diminished by his bluntness and exaggeration (TRB, 1989). Further, Bennett was diverted from dealing with drug abuse as a national problem by the necessity of addressing a drug-fed crime wave in Washington, D.C. (Miller, 1989)—a situation not unique to that city, however (Hackett, 1989).

There were constitutional issues involved in attempts to deal with drug abuse as well. Authorities intent on gaining acceptance and approval for their antidrug strategies were impeded by a number of aggressive, if not overzealous and excessive, initiatives (Morganthau, 1990). Federal authorities began vigorously to apply Continuing Criminal Enterprise (CCE) and Racketeer Influenced and Corrupt Organizations (RICO) statutes to cases of suspected drug trafficking, undertaking assets seizures and forfeitures and prosecuting suspected traffickers for money laundering (Dombrink & Meeker,

1986). In the spirit of "zero tolerance," a policy under which any use of illegal drugs is considered to be a violation of the law that should be vigorously prosecuted, the secretary of the Department of Housing and Urban Development called for the eviction of suspected drug dealers from public housing projects ("Evicting the Drug Dealers," 1989). This denial of benefits based on *suspected* criminal behavior raised constitutional questions. In addition, state attorneys in many jurisdictions threatened to prosecute drug-using pregnant women (Gest, 1989), although few actually did (Board of Trustees, 1990; Hansen, 1992). Further, Bennett, the former head of the Department of Education, requested an end to federal aid for colleges that failed to punish drug-abusing students (DeLoughry, 1989), specifically targeting Pell Grant recipients (Jaschik, 1989).

Some supporters of the vigorous federal antidrug effort were nevertheless apprehensive about its implementation (Goldstein & Kalant, 1990; Marwick, 1989; "Speaking Out," 1989). A common theme among would-be supporters was that the policy, insofar as it addressed "demand reduction," was still dealing primarily with symptoms rather than causes of substance abuse and drug-related crime (Wilson & DiIulio, 1989). It was noted that many drug users, even if arrested for possession or sale of illegal substances, needed treatment more than prosecution and incarceration. Some observed that the defining line between "users" and "pushers/dealers" or "users/dealers"—the latter groups being recommended as key targets for law enforcement by many (Pearson, 1989)—was often hard to draw in practice.

Then there were the decriminalization/legalization debates. Some responded to the sea of doubt and frustration with recommendations for decriminalization of drug use (removal of criminal penalties for possession) or outright legalization (abolition of laws that prohibit production, sale, and distribution as well as possession) of either selected or all currently illicit drugs. Although these advocates were "an infinitesimally small minority" (Inciardi, 1992a), many were highly respected in their professional fields, and their opinions were published in such respected periodicals as *Public Interest, New Republic, Milbank Quarterly, Nature, National Review, New Perspectives Quarterly, Science,* and *Vital Speeches* (see, e.g., Bennett, Jackson, & Schmoke, 1989; Buckley, 1988; Cowan, 1986; Levine & Reinarman, 1991; Moore, 1991; Nadelmann, 1988a, 1988b, 1989; Sterling, 1991; Trebach & Englesman, 1989).

The scientific literature carried a number of careful, more neutral discussions of the decriminalization and legalization issues (see, e.g.,

Covington, 1987; Marshall, 1988). Official government comment understandably was unequivocally opposed (Bennett, 1990; Sessions, 1989), and the public at large appeared to be "solidly against legalization" (Inciardi, 1992a). Well-reasoned and -documented counterarguments (Clayton, 1989; Inciardi, 1991) soon began to debunk what most professionals in the field felt were superficial, ill-conceived, albeit largely well-intentioned ideas (see also Bayer, 1991; "Decriminalizing Drugs?" 1993; Kane, 1992; "Panacea or Chaos?" 1994).

As the use of crack cocaine increased and the news media competed for sensational headlines about its impacts, every holder or aspirant to public office was obliged to offer his or her recipe for a solution. In an article in *Newsweek,* Aric Press (1986) listed what he called "the Forthright Politician's Guide to Drug Enforcement," which included recommendations for more police on the streets and more arrests, more jail terms, less use of plea bargaining, life imprisonment for crack dealers, and the death penalty for some drug pushers. Press is credited with using the phrase "the criminal justice equivalent of bulimia" to describe the process whereby the police go on an arrest binge and then, "overwhelmed and overfed, the rest of the system—prosecutors, defenders, judges and jailers—[spends] its days in an endless purge, desperately trying to find ways to move its population before it gets hit with another wave tomorrow" (quoted in Wilson & DiIulio, 1989).

Similarly, judicial leaders pointed out that this "desperate" situation in the courts was caused by the actions of other branches of government:

> The ability of the courts to perform their role well is greatly affected by executive and legislative branch policies and programs. The executive branch, through its law enforcement agencies, determines how many alleged offenders will be arrested and prosecuted. The legislative branch determines which activities will be proscribed, sets limits upon the exercise of judicial sentencing and juvenile disposition power, and appropriates the resources that establish court capacity. (Lipscher, 1989, p. 14)

Without question, the war on drugs had overburdening effects on the criminal justice system. By 1990, the annual total of arrests for drug abuse violations reported by local and state law enforcement agencies surpassed 1 million (Shannon, 1989). This volume was 70% higher than in 1981—90% higher among those 18 years and older. This was not simply the result of population growth; total arrests increased only

31% in this same period. More than two-thirds of the arrests in 1990 involved possession charges; one-third of the arrests were for possession of "heroin or cocaine and their derivatives" (U.S. Department of Justice, 1991). In the federal system, there was a 74% increase in the number of persons prosecuted for drug offenses between 1980 and 1987 (U.S. Department of Justice, 1989).

The federal courts began to feel drug case pressure early on during the war on drugs, as policies focused on prosecutions of higher-level traffickers and dealers, international sales, and multistate distribution networks. Gest (1990) notes that Congress and the Bush administration had directed much of federal antidrug funding to support federal rather than state prosecutions. Eventually, drug cases would account for 44% of federal criminal trials and almost half of federal criminal appeals. Almost a quarter of a million federal criminal drug cases were reported to be on file in 1990. Civil suits still outnumbered felony cases in the federal courts, but the criminal caseload rose 59% during the 1980s, and drug cases soared by 280% (whereas civil cases rose by just 39%). But, as Turque (1989) has noted, "the hard line on the street has not been matched by an investment in additional jails and courts" (pp. 36-37).

In April 1989, a national conference was convened in Philadelphia by judicial leaders from the nine most populous states. The general consensus among those at the conference was that most trial courts were being overwhelmed by drug cases (Lipscher, 1989, p. 14). The conferees reported feelings of desperation caused by backlogs and delays in court processing as well as shortages of jail and prison space. They expressed concern that this situation undermined deterrence and bred contempt for the law, and warned of dire consequences—caseload crisis or even system breakdown—if solutions were not soon found (Lipscher, 1989, p. 15). In short, the conferees were generally pessimistic regarding the ability of court systems or liaison systems such as TASC to handle *any* of their responsibilities effectively as a result of drug and criminal case overload ("Panel Presentation," 1990).

Perhaps most visible in the movement to ease the stress on the courts has been Judge Jeffery S. Tauber, the founder of Oakland's court diversion program for drug-involved offenders and president of the recently formed National Association of Drug Court Professionals. Judge Tauber noted in 1993:

Judges are in a unique position to exert effective leadership in the promotion of coordinated drug control efforts, both within the criminal justice system and their local communities. Judges have the political influence, the ties to government agencies, the moral authority, the perceived fairness and impartiality, and the expertise and focus necessary to bring leadership to coordinated antidrug efforts.

Traditionally, judges have played the passive role of objective, impartial referee, only reluctantly stepping beyond the boundaries of their own courtroom. However, where the fair and effective administration of justice is threatened (as in this case by an exploding drug problem), the court has the responsibility to come forward and become a leader and active participant in the organization, design and implementation of coordinated criminal justice and community-wide drug control efforts. (p. 4)

The Emergence of Drug Courts

By the end of the 1980s, many courts had concluded that all previous reforms and liaisons with drug treatment programs intended to reduce delays had been exhausted. Cooper and Trotter (1994) report that courts increasingly "have begun to introduce methods for differentiating the management of drug cases to permit use of a variety of case-processing mechanisms, varying in applicable procedures, events, time frames, and judicial system resources, which can be adapted to the individual characteristics of cases files and litigants involved" (p. 84). These strategies, popularly known as drug courts, can be characterized as recognizing that traditional case processing strategies have been unresponsive to the special characteristics of many drug-dependent individuals, particularly in deterring the repetitive criminal behavior characteristic of drug-involved offenders and in addressing the medical, social, economic, and other problems associated with drug dependency (see Belenko, 1990; Belenko, Fagan, & Chin, 1991).

Relatively early drug court efforts focused on case processing management or "differentiated case management" (DCM) concepts. The latter emphasize optimum use of available judicial system resources by varying their allocation to different classes of cases based on management needs and the degree of judicial supervision required for their resolution. Segregated courts, which handle only felony drug cases and seek quick felony pleas, sometimes through offers of more lenient sanctions, gained early support as a reasonable case management tactic. However, these courts had their detractors, even within the criminal justice system ("Real Justice," 1992).

Specialization was seen as a means of rapidly developing processing expertise, new rules promoting pleas, and, consequently, efficiency.

Eliminating competition with violent felonies in general court calendars was felt to result in fewer postponements and to allow the courts to deal with more "serious" cases. Most cases were generated by street-level antidrug enforcement efforts, which tended to have strong evidence and reliable witnesses. This reduced the likelihood that defendants would seek trial and minimized the case preparation and investigative processes for prosecutors (Belenko, Fagan, & Dumanovsky, 1994, p. 55).

As Smith, Davis, and Goretsky (1991, p. 7) note, case processing management was designed to expedite those cases that in all likelihood will not result in a trial and to release court resources to handle cases that do result in trials and appeals. The premise is that where attorneys and judges are required to handle cases quickly and consistently, with a structured schedule for completion of each phase of the litigation, defendants and victims will be more justly served and courts will be able to proceed smoothly. A case flow management system encourages timely movement from filing to disposition and allows for red flags when attorneys lag behind or cases go awry. Progress can be monitored readily, and courts are able to see quickly where the system bogs down, so that they are able to "troubleshoot" more expediently.

A common theme among these variations, and a key feature that merits the use of the term *innovative* to describe these court reforms, is the requirement of true collaboration among elements of the criminal justice system that traditionally have emphasized autonomy. Moreover, in many jurisdictions, local private and public human services agencies are involved in the collaboration as well. This collaboration, together with the innovative procedures and programs developed, reflects a fundamental rethinking of the judicial function and the role that the court and the judiciary can play in controlling drug abuse. Rather than relying on organizations such as TASC or probation to identify, assess, refer, and monitor drug-using offenders, drug court judges act as case managers.

The First Drug Courts

Belenko and Dumanovsky (1993) cite New York City as the first jurisdiction to use special drug courts in the early 1970s. They point to virtual emergency strategies that were necessary to deal with massive numbers of arrests following enactment of the harsh so-called Rockefeller Drug Laws.[2] With changes in these laws, and particularly with reductions in their enforcement, the New York

City courts gradually reverted to mixed-calendar courts to deal with rising numbers of nondrug felony cases. Then, in 1987, new "Narcotics Parts" drug courts were set up in four of New York City's five boroughs in response to rising numbers of crack cocaine and other felony drug cases. The primary goal was to speed case disposition by instituting a process whereby defendants waive their rights to a grand jury hearing and combined the functions of the superior and lower courts in allowing judges to accept pleas to misdemeanors or felonies (Belenko et al., 1994).

Since the first steps taken in New York, state and local courts that incorporate drug abuse treatment as a prominent goal in the adjudication process have generated considerable interest among both justice system practitioners and treatment providers. Tauber (1994) has stated (in what may be something of an exaggeration) that interest in drug courts is "sweeping the nation" (p. 28). It bears repeating that this type of court is not the only type that can legitimately call itself a "drug court," although it may be the model that most people understand when they hear the term. To reiterate, drug courts are courts specifically designated to administer cases referred for judicially supervised drug treatment and rehabilitation within a jurisdiction or court-enforced drug treatment programs (Casey, 1994, p. 118).

The jurisdiction serving Miami (Dade County), Florida, is generally identified as the first court to break new ground as a drug court in two respects: The sentencing judge, rather than a probation officer, monitors offender progress, and defendants are usually allowed to stay in the program even when they violate its conditions of participation. The program was initiated in July 1989, and "court experts throughout the country have touted the Miami drug treatment program; it has also been featured on a number of national television news programs" (Davis, Smith, & Lurigio, 1994, p. 4) and in numerous published newsmagazine articles. The original focus of the Miami program was diversion to treatment of defendants charged with possession of drugs (not sales) who had no prior felony convictions.

A host of factors can be cited as stimuli for the creation of the Miami drug court:

1. recognition that for some time, 70% of the capital cases being considered by the grand jury had been drug related;
2. drug-related deaths, accidents, and arrests involving well-known and successful persons;

3. local medical examiner reports of a large and puzzling increase in cocaine-induced deaths involving apparently small amounts of ingested cocaine;

4. a study that confirmed and quantified that a majority of arrestees entering the local criminal justice system had been recent users of cocaine; and

5. analysis of case processing data that produced the conclusion that too many people who were known to be in need of treatment for cocaine use were being released from custody with "credit time served," with no "carrots or sticks" to press them toward treatment services (K. F. Rundle, personal communication, July 13, 1993).

Temple University researcher John Goldkamp (1994) notes that the numbers of reported crimes and adult arrests had risen steadily in the late 1980s in the Miami drug court jurisdiction. Adult arrests had increased by 45% and arrests for drug possession had increased by 93% between 1985 and 1989. Goldkamp further reports that a study of 1987 felony defendants in this jurisdiction found that approximately 73% tested positive for cocaine at arrest processing, and approximately 83% of all arrests could be classified as drug related.

Flicker (1990, p. 64) cites data from a jail survey conducted in 1988 that portrayed the "main jail" (Miami Metropolitan Corrections Center) as having a population of 1,065, although the facility's rated capacity was 424—the jail was 152% over capacity. However, Flicker's data pale into insignificance when compared with information reported by Viglucci (1992) 2 years later; by then, the midyear population of the facility was 1,950 and had been as high as 2,200. A decade-old federal court order against the county to reduce jail overcrowding was raising anxiety because, despite spending $72 million since 1987 for jail improvements and capacity expansion, the jail system was as congested as ever at more than 6,000 inmates. The main jail was worse, and the county budget was reeling under annual corrections department operating budgets that ballooned from $37 million to $82 million over a 5-year period.

Other Drug Court Implementations

Other jurisdictions identified as having "management-oriented" drug courts that use case processing "tracks" are located in Los Angeles, Detroit, St. Joseph (Berrien County, Michigan), and Philadelphia. Jurisdictions cited as having special court divisions with a similar emphasis, most of which are said to use expedited drug case processing procedures, are located in Milwaukee, San Antonio, Loredo (Webb County, Texas), Charlotte, Baltimore, Wilmington (New Castle County, Delaware), New Brunswick (Middlesex County, New Jersey), Portland, and Washington, D.C. Other jurisdictions with "management" orientation variants are located in Chicago, Dallas, El Paso, and Fort Worth (Cooper & Trotter, 1994, pp. 87-90). This list can be considered to be partial, for reasons discussed elsewhere in this chapter.

Among the areas that have since instituted deferred prosecution drug courts are Los Angeles and Oakland, Pensacola (Florida), Kalamazoo (Michigan), Kansas City, Las Vegas, Portland, Beaumont and Austin (Texas), Baltimore, and Tallahassee. Deferred prosecution as a component of a broader case management-oriented program has been reported in St. Joseph (Michigan), Mobile, and Wilmington (Delaware). Postdisposition programs that feature substance abuse treatment have been implemented in Ft. Lauderdale, Phoenix, and Washington, D.C. Most of these programs target first offenders who do not have serious records; the Kalamazoo program targets female offenders who, if convicted, would be subject to mandatory incarceration (Cooper & Trotter, 1994, pp. 95-96).

As can be seen, simple descriptions and groupings of drug courts are difficult, because no two courts are exactly alike (Casey, 1994; Cooper & Trotter, 1994, p. 94; Davis et al., 1994, p. 1). A number of factors, including judicial and financial resources, available courthouse facilities, constituent support, and commitment from treatment providers, contribute to the nature of particular programs' success. The local "legal culture"—that is, the shared expectations, practices, and informal rules of behavior of judges and attorneys (Church, Carlson, Lee, & Tan 1978)—represents a cluster of intangible factors clearly related to how a drug court becomes implemented and institutionalized in a particular jurisdiction.

The sources and means used by individual jurisdictions to fund drug courts are as varied as the structures and operational details among drug court descriptions. Although the published literature is virtually mute on this point, it is reasonable to conclude, based upon the collective presentations and informal remarks offered at the First National Drug Court Conference in 1993, that jurisdictions are overwhelmingly reliant on local financial support. The following two examples are illustrative.

In 1991, Judge Stanley Goldstein of the well-known Miami drug court suggested to the director-designate of the Office of National Drug Control Policy (the federal "drug czar"):

The [drug court] concept works, and it ought to be encouraged at the national level by the new czar. I think there should be some form of drug court in every jurisdiction to divert people with drug problems out of an overcrowded system. By throwing first-time drug offenders in jail, you're only making criminals out of them and wasting tax dollars. The feds should see to it that these types of programs are funded. As it stands, we have to pray for grants. We pray and we beg and we do whatever we can to find money. ("Advice for the New Drug Czar," 1991)

The Miami drug court program, with a reported average annual operating budget of some $1.6 million for its Drug Abuse Treatment Program for fiscal years 1990-1992, receives major support ($1 million) from the Dade County General Fund. The county is reported to have derived these funds by developing a new method of redistributing income from traffic offense fees. The treatment program is also reported to return proceeds from client fees assessed according to a sliding scale to the General Fund in amounts ranging from $132,000 to $276,000 annually (Finn & Newlyn, 1993a, pp. 19-20; 1993b, p. 13).

Contemporary Drug Courts: The Judge as Case Manager

Judge Jeffery Tauber is the originator of the Oakland (Piedmont and Emeryville, California) Municipal Court drug court, which has served as a model for drug courts in many other areas. He has described the major guiding principles for his drug court in various presentations and published accounts. The following summary, drawn from his work, provides a conceptual picture of what goes on in many drug treatment courts.

In a drug court, communication between judge and offender is crucial. By increasing the frequency of court hearings as well as the intensity and length of judge-offender contacts, the drug court judge becomes a powerful motivator for the offender's rehabilitation. Drug court judges hold hearings before an audience full of offenders. As appropriate, judges assume the roles of confessor, taskmaster, cheerleader, and mentor. They exhort, threaten, encourage, and congratulate participants for their progress or lack thereof. The court hearing is used to educate the audience as well as the individual offender on the potential consequences of the program. Offenders who have failed the program are seen early in the hearing before a full audience of participants; successful graduates are often handed

diplomas by the judge, accompanied by the applause and congratu-
lations of staff.

Effective drug court programs are based on an understanding of
the physiological, psychological, and behavioral realities of drug
abuse and are implemented with those realities in mind. Court-
ordered drug rehabilitation programs have the task of dispelling the
generally held belief that "nothing works" in treating drug offenders.
This untrue perception becomes a self-fulfilling prophecy when
financially strapped communities inadequately fund court-ordered
treatment programs and skeptical judges halfheartedly implement
those programs, often terminating participants at the first sign of
drug relapse.

There are a few important "reality-based principles" shared by
many of the drug courts implemented to date. These include immediate, up-front intervention; coordinated, comprehensive supervision; long-term treatment and aftercare; and progressive sanctions
and incentive programs.

Contingency contracting is the structural cornerstone of some
programs. A contingency contract sets out the standards of and
consequences for offender conduct during the program. Developed
collaboratively by all key players, the objectives of such a contract
are to ensure that the offender's behaviors are rewarded or penalized;
to provide ground rules for the offender, to reduce confusion during
program implementation and operations; to promote program sta-
bility and effectiveness by developing coordination and collaboration through the consensual decision-making process; to make the
offender accountable for his or her behavior; and to give the offender
control over his or her own rehabilitation, ultimately making the
offender a participant rather than a self-described victim of the
rehabilitation program (Tauber, 1994).

As described by John Goldkamp (1994), a courtroom-based team
approach—particularly a central, hands-on judicial role—distinguishes
the Miami drug court model from other drug court initiatives. The
courtroom environment of the Miami Felony Drug Court "has been
described by Dade County's Executive Assistant Public Defender as
a 'theater in the square' " because it departs from the normal criminal
courtroom in several respects (p. 113). The major distinguishing
difference is in the role of the judge. The Miami drug court judge
presides over many brief hearings regarding defendant entry into the
program, in-court progress reports, and graduation from treatment.
These hearings often involve sanctioning of program participants for
absconding or rearrests for new offenses. Sometimes the judge will

order the defendant confined to "motivational" jail time in an area reserved for drug court defendants, with the defendant's continuing participation to be reassessed after that period of confinement.[3] The judge also may transfer the cases of some defendants out of drug court to be tried in normal fashion by other circuit court felony judges.

Perhaps even more nontraditional are the roles performed by other Miami drug court officials, activities that have been described variously as "unorthodox," "nonadversarial," and "team oriented." Goldkamp (1994) has characterized courtroom transactions in the Miami drug court as sometimes more akin to "psychodrama" or "therapeutic community" treatment modalities than to normal criminal courtroom proceedings (p. 114). The prosecutor alternates between conveying strong encouragement to defendants who appear to be making progress and threatening to reinstate formal prosecution of charges when defendants' program participation reflects waning commitment. The defense counsel (usually a public defender) manifests an unequivocally favorable courtroom attitude regarding the opportunity provided by the drug court and also plays a role that appears more therapeutic than adversarial. Personnel representing treatment programs and pretrial services attend the hearings and update the judge, prosecutors, and defenders regarding outside-the-courtroom developments in each case (Goldkamp, 1994, pp. 113-114).[4]

The Miami and Oakland drug treatment courts are two that have been pioneers and are best known. There were other early innovators as well, and many have been developed since. As for the actual number of drug courts in the United States, there are more than 3,000 major trial courts or "courts of general jurisdiction" (also referred to as circuit, district, or superior courts), each of which conceivably could establish a drug court division or *court part*. How many actually have done so is difficult to ascertain, for a variety of reasons. First, the court-enforced drug treatment program model that seems to be of interest to many jurisdictions is of very recent vintage (a few "process-oriented" drug courts were created earlier). Second, most drug courts established to date have emerged as a result of local initiative and without centralized federal funding or registration. Third, the variety of programs that have been labeled drug courts (night courts, expedited processing, mixed calendar, diversion, and postsentence) complicate simple tabulations. And fourth, so many jurisdictions are in various stages of contemplation, planning, and implementation that any published tally would immediately be out of date.

It is possible, however, to derive a rough estimate of the number of drug courts by using projections from recent surveys. Milkman, Beaudin, Tarmann, and Landson (1992, 1993) report the results of a stratified random sample survey of 300 jurisdictions. Of the 264 jurisdictions that responded when contacted in their 1992 survey, drug courts were reported as being available in only 14%, and another 41% reported them as being desirable. Using these figures as a base, a projected drug court count for early 1992 would be approximately 420 nationwide, with more than 1,000 other jurisdictions considering them.

A review of the published list of attendees at the first National Drug Court Conference in December 1993 provides more recent data from which to infer active interest in the drug court concept. More than 100 jurisdictions were represented at this conference, of which 25 had already established drug courts (based upon information gleaned from conference presentations, informal interviews with participants, and collateral listings from materials distributed at the meeting). In a recent public forum, one of the conference leaders estimated that there may be currently 50 treatment-oriented drug courts in operation nationally.

Evaluations of Drug Courts

Rossi and Freeman (1993) define *evaluation research* as the systematic application of social research procedures to the assessment of the conceptualization, design, implementation, and utility of social intervention programs. They describe three major classes of evaluation research, and they apply the term *comprehensive evaluation* to studies that include all three types. Evaluations that focus on program conceptualization and design seek to clarify such issues as the nature and scope of the problem, where it is located and whom it affects, feasible interventions, and appropriate target populations for a particular intervention. Evaluations that emphasize monitoring and accountability of program implementation are interested primarily in whether the intervention is reaching the target population, is being managed and administered in the manner appropriate for human services programs, is properly accountable to sponsors and stakeholders, and is implemented and operated in the ways originally envisioned and designed. Finally, evaluations that concentrate on the assessment of program utility include studies that gauge both the degree to which a program produces the desired *outcomes (im-*

pact) and its *benefits in relation to its costs (efficiency)* in order to ascertain its *utility.*

Program Conceptualization and Design Issues

Evaluators have generally concluded that the initiation of drug courts has not included careful conceptual development. Those who have examined a number of these courts have concluded that the first step for any jurisdiction contemplating the creation of a drug court is the formation of an "interagency planning committee." Based on analysis of survey results, site observations, interviews, and meta-analysis of descriptive reports of the development of drug courts, Belenko and Dumanovsky (1993) recommend that such a committee include representatives from a jurisdiction's public defender and state attorney offices, corrections department, treatment providers, and executive branch (criminal justice coordinator or public safety commissioner), and that it be chaired by a judicial leader or court administrator.

Among the first tasks the interagency planning committee should tackle is a needs assessment (or systems analysis) of the local court, corrections department, and drug abuse treatment systems. The questions that require discussion include the following:

- What are the current drug and nondrug felony caseloads?
- What are the average times to disposition for drug and nondrug felony cases?
- What is the average caseload per judge?
- What are the current barriers to more rapid disposition times?

After evaluating the ability of the existing court system to dispose of felony drug cases, the planning committee must decide whether a special drug court is necessary or whether current caseloads can be absorbed through a general improvement in case management. The key questions at this point are as follows:

- What type of drug court is needed or desired?
- What, if any, are the existing diversion or alternatives to incarceration programs in the jurisdiction for drug-involved defendants?
- Should drug treatment be a key component of the court?
- Will the court function as a diversion or deferred prosecution program with cases dismissed or *nolled* following successful treatment completion?[5]

Assuming that the answers to the last two of these questions are affirmative, the committee should proceed to develop detailed plans that include realistic achievable objectives and goals. Few jurisdictions have surpluses of community-based treatment resources that can readily absorb the increased numbers of treatment referrals that drug courts promise to provide. Examples of critical questions to be asked at this point include the following:

- What is the current availability of drug treatment programs for criminal justice clients?
- Are there a variety of modalities and environments appropriate for the types of clients the drug court anticipates referring?
- Should the drug court attempt to develop a dedicated treatment provider or system devoted exclusively to receiving its referrals?
- Should defendant proximity to the courthouse be a primary treatment placement criterion (to improve probabilities of clients making their first appointments and ease of monitoring and court appearances)?
- Should acupuncture detoxification be provided and promoted as an adjunctive therapy to traditional treatment methods?[6]

The planning committee must assume that a variety of treatment needs will be identified and should address the question of how placement decisions will be made. For example:

- How will defendants be classified at an early point (based on estimated drug involvement and risk to public safety) to assist in the targeting of appropriate candidates and in planning for treatment and supervision?

All participants must "buy into" the drug court concept for it to achieve its goals. Explicit and detailed procedural rules of the drug court program help to define and achieve interagency cooperation. Success depends upon development of channels of open and ongoing communication to identify and resolve problems as they arise. Thus, as planning proceeds, the interagency committee should establish formal written procedural rules that cover such details as the following:

- Will defendants be required to plead guilty, waive their grand jury or speedy trial rights, or stipulate to the police arrest report before being adjudicated in the drug court?
- What will the procedures be for assigning cases in the drug court?
- What types of cases will be accepted—first offenders, nonviolent offenders, or all drug-involved offenders?

A major policy step in implementing any drug court program is the definition of the initial target population. Careful targeting can ensure that treatment resources will be deployed efficiently to process a sufficiently challenging group of defendants with no adverse impact on public safety. If sights are set too low—for example, if the court must deal with very minor offenders—program resources may easily be overwhelmed by the volume of cases. That is, diversion of defendants without extensive criminal histories who have been charged with relatively minor crimes carries the inherent risk of "widening the net" to include persons not usually processed by criminal courts, possibly unwittingly adding to court workload and jail population (Middleton, 1992). On the other hand, assessment findings might suggest defining the criteria for eligibility to include other types of drug-involved felony-level defendants who may not be charged with drug offenses (Goldkamp & Weiland, 1993a, p. 8).

Furthermore, another question that should be asked is this:

- What will the procedures be for maintaining cases in the drug court— procedures for responding to violations of court orders or treatment program rules, dirty urines,[7] and so on—and what rewards will be provided for achievements?

Rewards for offender/participant compliance and sanctions for noncompliance with the court's or treatment program's requirements should be specified and applied fairly and consistently. Sanctions can range from oral admonishments to short jail terms for failures.

The Miami drug court, one of the leading models, became notable partly because it was among the first to acknowledge explicitly high levels of program tolerance for the sorts of behavior likely to be associated with drug-involved individuals. This approach contrasts clearly with approaches that emphasize punishment for program missteps (Goldkamp & Weiland, 1993a). Consistent with this philosophy, Belenko and Dumanovsky (1993) recommend that participants receive acupuncture treatments to help ease their cravings for drugs and to help them relax, and to make them more amenable to the treatment intervention program, because failures usually occur early. They further recommend a drug court treatment program that allows participants to change their minds about pursuing treatment during the early phase and return to the standard adjudication route.

It is vital that strong judges be assigned to drug courts, those who are respected and dedicated to the principles of the special court and who are knowledgeable about substance abuse and treatment.

Obviously, they must be supported by their court administrators and chief judges (Belenko & Dumanovsky, 1993, p. 5). Teamwork in the courtroom notwithstanding, the leadership role of an actively involved judge who is familiar with drug-influenced behaviors is an essential element in a court's capacity to function well. The judge needs to be encouraging and supportive to defendants in the admission and progress review hearings, even when he or she finds it necessary to impose sanctions for poor performance or when the defendant has been returned to the drug court on an *alias capias* (Goldkamp & Weiland, 1993a).

Impact Evaluation and Cost-Efficiency Issues

Impact assessments are undertaken to determine whether or not interventions have produced their intended effects. They are typically designed as a compromise between two competing pressures: (a) the desire for rigor sufficient to reach relatively firm conclusions and (b) the design of options and methodological procedures that are limited by the practical considerations of time, money, cooperation, and protection of human subjects. Such investigations are relevant throughout the life course of social programs—in the formation stage, where there are policy debates; in pilot demonstrations, to measure outcome effects; during program design, to test for effective methods; after initial implementation, to prove a program's effectiveness before it is extended to some wider coverage; and/or during periods when program goals are revised in order to modify or enhance effectiveness (Rossi & Freeman, 1993, pp. 215-217).

Prerequisites of any assessment of impact include (a) well-articulated program objectives and (b) a sufficiently well implemented intervention. Assessment of a program's real effects is complicated and confounded by both extraneous and endogenous factors that must be minimized. Processes and events outside the researcher's control that are particularly difficult to deal with include (a) uncontrolled client selection (most commonly self-selection) resulting in some members of the target population being more likely than others to participate in the evaluated program and (b) "deselection" (dropping out), which works in the opposite direction to bring about differential attrition in program participation. Other factors favoring the selection of some clients into a program may not reflect motivations so much as opportunity or ability.

Drug courts of all types should be interested in their impact on recidivism. The most frequently used measures in this regard include

1. felony rearrest rates for both drug and nondrug crimes and
2. time to rearrest.

Treatment-oriented drug courts should examine defendant treatment performance, including the following:

3. proportions of clients completing treatment,
4. proportions requiring motivational jail time,
5. restarts required,[8] and
6. length of time to completion.

Some corrections system impacts that might be measured in drug court program evaluations include

7. jail/prison beds freed by drug court diversion and/or postsentence treatment in community-based facilities and
8. beds filled by motivational jail.

Because case processing is an area of major interest to most courts, drug court evaluations might also include these measures:

9. proportion of felony cases eligible for drug court,
10. proportion of eligible cases enrolling in program,
11. numbers of program entrants belatedly found to be ineligible and removed from the program,
12. changes in types of dispositions for drug cases,
13. time to disposition—for acceptance into program and/or to case closure,
14. processing efficiency for both drug and nondrug cases,
15. time lost in failures to appear, and
16. resources expended in processing bench warrants.

Given the inevitable condition of scarce resources, economic efficiency is almost always a critical consideration in policy making, planning, and program implementation decision making. Increasingly, knowledge of drug court impacts alone is insufficient; program results are usually judged against their costs. Even those with relatively favorable outcomes may not be supported if their costs are high relative to their impacts. Estimating impacts in comparison with costs is technically, and often politically/administratively, difficult, because it requires assignment of dollar values to all program-related activities and program benefits.

To date, cost-efficiency analyses of drug courts have been virtually nonexistent. When they have been conducted, some of the measures that have been likely to be used have included added expenses associated with operating courtrooms dedicated strictly or largely to drug court transactions, costs not covered by client fees associated with providing treatment, missed appearances, program misstarts, costs of motivational jail, savings in case processing, savings in jail/prison confinement (pretrial, postconviction), and savings from lowered/slowed reoffense rates.

Chicago Drug Night Courts

Cook County, Illinois, was the first jurisdiction in the United States to implement a night drug court in an attempt to alleviate stress on courtroom space arising from significant increases in drug case filings. Essentially, Chicago court authorities added evening shifts in five courtrooms (later expanded to eight) and dedicated the calendars of these night courts to felony drug cases. The U.S. Bureau of Justice Assistance provided funds to the American Bar Association and Loyola University of Chicago to conduct an evaluation study of this court. The evaluators used interviews, records data, and on-site observations of night court operations. Their summarized findings can be categorized into two broad areas: efficiency and the quality of justice (see Smith et al., 1991; Smith, Davis, & Goretsky, 1993; Smith, Lurigio, Davis, Elstein, & Popkin, 1994).

Inefficiencies noted include the fact that supervision of night court operations is difficult because most criminal justice agency administrative staff work day shifts; overflow cases cannot be shifted when an evening's calendar is finished early; and getting information essential to adjudicating cases is perceived by staff to be more difficult at night. Many efficiencies were also noted, however: 9,700 cases were disposed of in the first year of operation, significantly surpassing the target of 5,000; median time to disposition—from case assignment to sentencing—fell from 245 to 86 days; and the number of court dates per drug case dropped from about 11 to 6.

Staff-related quality-of-justice issues included staff and judge fatigue associated with rapid case processing and the nighttime schedule; caseload pressures that interfered with staff members' and judges' perceived abilities to do their jobs well; security, both within the building and in transit to/from work; reduced time that staff and judges had to spend with their families because of the night-shift work (70% of the night court workers stated a preference for daytime work even though most were nominally "volunteers"); and the intimation that night court staff were less qualified than other court workers, inherent in the suggestion that staff rotations and incentives might be necessary "to obtain staff with qualifications equal to day court operations."

Procedure-related quality-of-justice issues noted were as follows: As feared by public defenders, there was a decrease of 10 percentage points in cases represented by private counsel after the night courts began; plea rates increased significantly, whereas dismissal and bench trial rates fell proportionally (the jury trial rate did not decline significantly); there were no changes in the rate of filings of suppression and other motions by defense counsels; convicted offenders sentenced to probation rose from 45% to 67%, whereas periods of probation decreased significantly; and sentences involving drug treatment for narcotics offenders remained infrequent (4%) and unchanged after drug night courts were established. This last finding was attributed by the researchers to two primary factors: (a) Probation sentences for drug defendants contain few incentives to volunteer for TASC-managed treatment (which requires participants to be treatment motivated), and (b) TASC will not accept defendants charged with drug sales. The presiding judge reported that there are few simple possession cases in the Chicago jurisdiction, which is consistent with Wice's (1994) report that in the New Brunswick, New Jersey, drug court, an estimated "90 percent of the trials in the drug court involved this solitary issue: possession or sale" (p. 43).

The investigators reported that some local authorities they interviewed felt that, by segregating drug cases, drug courts in general dispense "assembly-line justice," "routinize" case processing at the expense of defendants' rights, encourage "tunnel vision"—limiting the judge's ability to evaluate drug cases in the context of other crimes—and tend toward "canned" offers that can work against individual attention to cases. Some of the local critics argued that innocent defendants chose the typically light sentences (involving only probation) and that those on probation seldom received drug abuse treatment, often being returned to court to have their probation sentences revoked for violations and to be sentenced to prison. The researchers' conclusions seem to support the concerns of the Chicago court critics:

> By setting up new courts, staffing them with new judges, and introducing better case management practices, the judicial administration successfully overcame the inertia built into the system. Processing drug cases

became far more efficient, but with some possible costs to the quality of justice. (Smith, Lurigio, et al., 1994, p. 51)

The New York City N-Part Drug Courts

The Manhattan County (New York City) jurisdiction is credited with being the first (in early 1987) to set up "speedy disposition" drug courts. These "N- (Narcotic) Part" case management drug courts were later implemented in other New York City jurisdictions. Drug defendants were offered misdemeanor convictions with short jail terms, reduced felony charges, or shorter prison sentences for agreeing to a well-established felony waiver (to a grand jury hearing) process. The primary goal was to speed case disposition. One evaluation revealed that sharply reduced average case processing times were achieved in N-Parts (13.6 days) when compared with similar cases in regular courts (151.5 days). This study also found a higher rate of probation sentences in the N-Parts (Belenko, Davis, & Dumanovsky, 1992).

Belenko et al. (1994) note that there have been policy and ethical questions about whether rational and fair dispositions could be achieved in a relatively brief time under the N-Parts. They also raise some questions about the risks to public safety posed by the N-Parts' higher rate of probation sentences. They address this issue by suggesting that if recidivism were comparable or even less for drug offenders sentenced to probation supervision, public safety would not be jeopardized by the N-Parts' "leniency." Using a retrospective matched comparison group design, Belenko et al. chose two final samples of 2,758 N-Parts cases and 3,225 from other courts. After extensive analysis, they conclude in their summarized findings, "Even after controlling for prior drug charges and prior punishment, there appeared to be no strong or consistent [rearrest] effects associated with the rapid case processing or more lenient punishment imposed within this specialized drug court" (p. 76). Belenko et al. acknowledge that their analyses beg the question of quality of justice in specialized drug courts, noting that emphasis on processing speed is a particular concern in jurisdictions (such as the one studied) where full and early discovery is not the norm.

The Expedited Drug Case Management Courts

During the mid-1980s, researchers found that courts varied dramatically in the time devoted to case processing, for reasons unrelated to the drug epidemic. The fastest courts were found to take one-tenth the time to dispose of cases as the slowest. The differences were not attributable to court size or caseload per judge, but to caseload management. Courts with speedier processing tended (a) to maintain strict case processing standards; (b) to use management information effectively and to maintain tight administrative control over litigation pace; (c) to screen and track cases at the time of charging, using experienced prosecutors; (d) to assign defense counsel early; (e) to produce criminal history, laboratory, and presentence reports quickly; and (f) to have mechanisms for the speedy resolution of motions and acceptance of pleas.

The Bureau of Justice Assistance provided funding in 1988 for six jurisdictions to implement such procedures under a DCM program. In July 1989, three jurisdictions were funded to implement variants of this model under an "expedited drug case management" (EDCM) program. The focus was drug case processing, and the model was expanded to include linkages to a treatment and supervision component. Overviews and program summaries of EDCM projects in Philadelphia, New Brunswick, and Indianapolis have been presented by Cooper, Solomon, Bakke, and Lane (1991), and evaluation reports on these projects are discussed by Jacoby, Ratledge, and Gramckow (1992).

Jacoby (1994) provides an update on the earlier evaluation reports of EDCM sites. To summarize, the EDCM program was never implemented in Indianapolis, primarily because of "the absence of an organizational infrastructure in the court to operate the program" (p. 29). In Philadelphia, arraignment and trial courts' organization made it necessary to process all felony cases through the program, making it look more like a DCM program with five tracks. The reported results included substantial decreases in average days from arraignment to disposition (from 166 to 119 days) and from disposition to sentence (from 31 to 19 days); an 18% increase in guilty pleas, 42% decrease in jury trials, and 28% reduction in dismissals and other dispositions; an increase in disposition rate, from 66% to 79%; and a 36% reduction in average number of jail days spent pretrial. In New Brunswick, a separate drug court was established de facto because the chief judge handled all drug cases. The only change Jacoby reports for this EDCM project is a 74% decrease (1989-1990) in average days to disposition from case initiation (from 241 to 81 days), in contrast to virtually no change in the same period for drug cases tried in all other Middlesex County courts (195 and 191 days).

The New Brunswick project is particularly interesting because it is the subject of another published evaluative report that provides a different perspective from Jacoby's. According to Wice (1994), the New Brunswick project was designed to operate in three tracks. Track A included drug cases with mandatory presumptive incarceration or a high probability of incarceration, such as those involving school zones, use of juveniles for distribution, first- or second-degree felonies, and prior convictions. Track B was for drug cases with no mandatory sentences and where long custodial sentences were a low probability, such as simple possession, intent to distribute but amount seized was small or defendant had no significant prior record, and factually or legally weak cases. Track C cases were those that could not be negotiated and were slated to go to the grand jury for possible trial. The goals for Tracks A and C were disposition within 90 days; the goal for Track B was 30 days.

For Track B defendants, the Middlesex model provided a community treatment component that Wice describes as relying heavily upon volunteers from the community. The 50-member Community Advisory Committee for New Brunswick provided oversight for this component, using court-approved policies and experienced court-designated liaisons. The committee operated through subcommittees for monitoring, restitution, coordination, public relations, education, and job placement. Wice reports that the last two of these subcommittees were "slow in developing and did not become operational during the first nine months of the drug court's existence" (p. 44) and that "there is a serious shortage of treatment facilities and services, but the overall performance appears successful" (p. 35).

This account provides no data regarding enrollments of Track B defendants in community-based substance abuse treatment programs. Wice reports that university student interns assisted volunteers in operating the urine monitoring program. He describes the outpatient counseling programs as short-term and staffed primarily by paraprofessionals with limited experience, "but it is a start and should only improve with age" (p. 45). Wice's discussion of the "treatment" component centers on descriptions of monitoring and restitution functions. Program participants were assigned to volunteer monitors who regularly checked on their attendance in treatment, work, or school, and their provision of urine specimens on schedule. Noted infractions were reported to probation officers, which resulted in defendants' being arrested and immediately brought before the court for revocation hearings. Volunteers also monitored the community service performance of defendants, who were required to wear bright orange vests imprinted with the words "community service." A Jefferson Institute report noted that there were a number of problems with the program, including judicial burnout, deficient program planning, too rapid expansion, insufficient administrative staff, and inefficient monitoring (Jefferson Institute for Justice Studies, 1992, p. 47).

Drug Treatment Courts

In an early evaluative study of the Miami drug court, Smith et al. (1991) report that what began as a "controlled experiment" in July 1989 had grown into a well-established program, but there was some concern that the counselors' caseloads were becoming too large for them to provide individual attention, and participants were not monitored as closely as originally intended. In addition, clients were not finishing the treatment program within the projected 1-year period, but were stretching the treatment to 18 months or longer. Despite these reservations, prosecutors, judges, public defenders, and the treatment staff enthusiastically supported the concept and were convinced that the drug court had been far more successful than they had anticipated.

Measures used to examine the effects of the drug court included (a) outcomes of drug cases before and after the drug court started, (b) outcomes of nondrug cases before and after the drug court began (to see whether processing [dispositions] of these cases was affected), (c) case processing time for drug and nondrug cases, and (d) recidivism data for drug offenders processed through the drug court compared with those handled by the general courts in the traditional manner. Findings included the following: Dispositions in drug cases changed significantly; percentages of cases resulting in "no action," probation, and jail declined, yet fewer than half of the cases assigned to the court successfully completed the treatment program and were *nolled*; dispositions of nonnarcotics cases shifted only slightly and nonsignificantly; case processing time increased dramatically, from a median number of days to disposition before the drug court of 49 to 366 days after the drug court began (there was no effect on processing time for nondrug cases).

The study data show only a small and statistically nonsignificant decrease in felony rearrests when defendants whose cases were assigned to drug court are compared with similar defendants whose cases were disposed prior to the establishment of the drug court. About 20% of the drug court defendants were rearrested for drug offenses and 32% were rearrested for any felony offenses within a year of the sampled arrest, compared with 23% and 33%, respectively, for pre-drug court defendants. This finding was at variance with local drug court-generated figures to the effect that the recidivism rate (as measured by rearrest in Dade County) for first-time drug offenders who successfully completed the drug court was only 7%, compared with 60% for similar offenders before the drug court.

Smith and his colleagues were quick to qualify their Miami drug court findings. Dade County was different from the other three courts studied because its goal was not to speed up the disposition of drug cases (indeed, it deliberately slowed the disposition by using diversion coupled with treatment in these cases), but to break the cycle of drug use and recidivism. The researchers' conclusions were of necessity based on all defendants assigned to drug court, not just the one-third to one-half who actually entered the treatment program. If the treatment program did have effects, they would have been "diluted" in the comparison. Smith et al. acknowledge a methodological shortcoming of not taking into account "time at risk," that is, not discounting for time spent in detention pretrial or postconviction in measuring rearrests. They note that they had no data to measure the court's impact on stopping the use of drugs by offenders, but that the rearrest data they did have indicated no significant reduction in felony rearrests following the introduction of the drug court (Smith et al., 1991).[9]

Postscript

How drug courts will proliferate and endure is difficult to predict. However, in August 1994, Congress passed and President Clinton signed the Violent Crime Control and Law Enforcement Act of 1994. This legislation authorized (as distinct from *appropriated*) $30.2 billion for anticrime programs to be created over a 6-year period ending in fiscal year 2000. The aspect of this legislation of greatest interest is that of Title V, Part V, which authorizes creation of a program of grants and other assistance to implement drug court programs. These programs are slated to combine intensive probation, supervision, and mandatory drug testing and treatment as alternative punishment for specified defendants. The eligibility criteria contained in the legislation limit participation to nonviolent drug-involved offenders (not charged with or convicted of offenses in which the person carried, possessed, or used a firearm or dangerous weapon, death or serious bodily injury ensued, or force was used against another person) and "first-time" drug offenders (having no prior convictions for felony crimes of violence involving the use or attempted use of force against a person with the intent to cause death or serious bodily harm).

States, state courts, local courts, units of local government, and Native American tribal governments are eligible to apply for and be awarded grants. Specifically, grants will fund programs that include mandatory periodic testing for the use of controlled substances or other addictive substances during any period of supervised release or probation for each participant; substance abuse treatment for each participant; diversion, probation, or other supervised release involving the possibility of prosecution, confinement, or incarceration, based on noncompliance with program requirements or failure to show satisfactory progress; and programmatic offender management and aftercare services, such as relapse prevention, health care, education, vocational training, job placement, and child care or other family support services for each participant who requires such services.

Although the passage of the crime bill would appear to bode well for the future of drug courts, the election of a Republican majority to the House and Senate at the close of 1994 represents a threat to aspects of the bill slated for rehabilitation programs. The change in Congress came, moreover, on the heels of some negative publicity about the much-touted Miami drug court. A series of articles in the *Miami Herald* on "crime and punishment" ran with the front-page subhead "Court Favored by Felons" and carried the following lead sentences:

> America is on the verge of making a $1 billion bet: that Miami's acclaimed Drug Court concept will help reduce crime in cities around the nation. But it hasn't done that in Miami. (Leen & Van Natta, 1994a)

In an accompanying article, *Herald* writers asked: "Is the program working? Who knows?" Furthermore, they censured court administrators for having failed to keep track of program participants, for not keeping accurate records, for admitting "violent felons" into the drug court, and for exaggerated claims of success (Leen & Van Natta, 1994b).

The *Miami Herald* articles purported to show how violent crime had become worse locally than virtually anywhere else in the country, and that many local judges were "soft" because they did not impose longer state prison sentences. The tone was largely "Let's get tougher on criminals," and the Miami drug court was targeted as symbolic of leniency and softness. The *Herald* message was clear:

> Begun as a program that sent first-time drug offenders to treatment instead of jail, Dade's Drug Court no longer resembles its national image or its idealistic beginnings. Slowly, over five years and without public notice, the Drug Court has become a loosely run assembly line that quickly moves hundreds of robbers and burglars off court calendars and back onto the streets in as little as 45 days. (Leen & Van Natta, 1994b)

But despite this negative publicity, the drug court concept is spreading across the country, buoyed by the strong support of President Clinton and Attorney General Janet Reno. The crime bill will invest $1 billion in new drug courts in cities all over the country. Already, 40 drug courts modeled after the Miami model have begun around the nation.

History is a compelling teacher. Experience demonstrates that progress against inertia is painfully slow, that momentum is precious, and that, once stalled, a program can take years to regain momentum. Therefore, it behooves all who believe that a comprehensive approach is the only reasonable hope of making significant progress against the broad and deep adverse consequences of drug abuse to actively resist simplistic, reactionary, and regressive policies. Drug courts—as means of organizing, "recruiting," and improving retention and outcomes in their associated rehabilitation programs—hold great promise, particularly with improvements in identification/selection, service needs assessment, case management, follow-up, and evaluation resources and practices. Properly planned, implemented, managed, and "institutionalized," drug courts can become integral components in an effective drug abuse intervention strategy. Toward this end, it appears crucial that drug courts and associated judges attempt to integrate their efforts with existing assessment, referral, and drug treatment programs. Clearly, there is strong momentum in the drug court movement. Its long-term success may depend on the integration of the drug court with capable liaison organizations, such as TASC, and experienced and successful local drug treatment programs. Such effective integration is important to the outcomes of this latest iteration of the relationship between the courts and drug treatment.

Notes

1. Some article titles that appeared in national newsmagazines illustrate the public sentiment: "Losing the War?" (Morganthau, 1988), "Crack: Hour by Hour, the Plague Feeds on Junkies and Cops, Hookers and Babies—and All of Us" (Adler, 1988), and "Tears of Rage: Americans Lose Patience With Panama and With a Failed Drug Policy" (Magnuson, 1988).

2. The so-called Rockefeller Laws of the 1970s were statutes targeting lower-level drug dealers. The results of these laws included a dramatic increase in the number of drug cases reaching the courts and the doubling of the time needed to dispose of them (Joint Committee on New York Drug Law Evaluation, 1977).

3. In some drug courts, the judge may remand program participants who violate or fail to follow drug treatment program rules (e.g., who fail to attend scheduled counseling sessions or submit too many "dirty" urine samples) to a number of days or weeks in jail in an attempt to "motivate" them to resume the program and abide by its rules.

4. For a more personalized, journalistic account of the proceedings in the Miami drug court, see Appendix A.

5. The *nolle prosequi* or *nol. pro.* is a formal entry into the record by which the prosecutor declares that he or she "will no further prosecute" a case as to some of the counts, as to some of the defendants, or altogether.

6. Acupuncture is a procedure involving the insertion of very fine needles into the skin at specific points with the intention of influencing bodily functions. This "art" or practice originated in ancient China; its popularization in the United States as an alternative medical approach has been attributed in part to media accounts of it during President Richard M. Nixon's historic visit to China in 1972. In 1975, Dr. Michael O. Smith in the Division of Substance Abuse at Lincoln Hospital in the Bronx, New York (which received many referrals from the criminal justice system), began to experiment with acupuncture as an alternative for methadone in heroin detoxification. He later extended its use to alcohol-abusing patients, then to cocaine and crack patients. In 1985, Dr. Smith founded the National Acupuncture Detoxification Association (NADA), and by the early 1990s acupuncture in addiction treatment had become popular with many in the criminal justice system, although many in the scientific, traditional Western medical and substance abuse treatment fields remain skeptical. A 1991 technical review by the National Institute on Drug Abuse concluded that there is no compelling evidence that acupuncture is an effective treatment for opiate or cocaine dependence. Nevertheless, this relatively inexpensive and easily expanded procedure has become a mainstay in a number of drug courts (Lowinson & Jaffe, 1995). Advocates of acupuncture detoxification point to observable behaviors during the needling sessions (relaxation to the point of sleep) and thereafter (reports of diminished craving for drugs, calmer individuals who are better able to participate in more traditional "talk therapies," and higher program retention rates) as evidence that the procedure "works."

7. *Dirty urines* is a colloquial term used by criminal justice and substance abuse treatment personnel to refer to urine specimens that have been found through chemical analysis (urinalysis) to contain (to test positive for) one or more illicit drugs. Urinalysis has been used sparingly within the treatment community for decades to verify suspected lapses among clients. Having dirty urines usually meant either that the clients were sanctioned within their treatment regimens or that they were

dismissed from the programs. Urinalysis technology was improved and popularized through a series of federally supported research projects in New York City and Washington, D.C., in the mid- to late 1980s. Urine testing began to be widely adopted in criminal justice settings as a means both of identifying drug users among arrested populations and of monitoring their urine specimens during the pretrial period to check for continuing use. Studies have demonstrated that such "urine surveillance" can reduce the rate of pretrial misconduct in general, including rearrest (Carver, 1986; Wish, 1990). The use of urine surveillance has been expanded in many jurisdictions to convicted populations under probation control, the reasoning being that it will provide an additional tool for officers and a deterrent to reoffending for probationers. Obviously, urine surveillance is a key component of most drug treatment courts, but concerns have been raised that the practice will come to replace counseling and other rehabilitative services where and when criminal justice systems have more drug-using offender referrals than local drug treatment resources can serve with appropriate types and levels of care.

8. Some drug court treatment programs penalize participants who have received motivational jail time or who have failed to show appropriate progress by "setting back" their treatment plans (and anticipated dates of completion) to earlier "phases" of the program. This retrogression may include a complete "restart" at the initial phase of the program.

9. The most comprehensive evaluation of the Miami drug court was undertaken by Goldkamp and Weiland (1993a, 1993b, 1993c). A full discussion of their design and findings appears in Appendix B of this book.

Appendix A

Proceedings in
the Miami Drug Court

MONDAY, 10:05 A.M. The judge who makes this court click gazes out over a crop of 60 recovering addicts, crack moms and lost septuagenarians whose mere presence rips holes in the image of cocaine as a young man's drug. They are like children to [the judge, who] has worked every corner of Dade's judicial system—from cop to defense attorney to prosecutor to judge—and finally arrived at his latest incarnation: a black-robed father figure, pep-talker and attitude-adjuster for people with three things in common: each used or bought drugs in Dade County; each got arrested for it; and each accepted a second chance.

The judge turns toward the fresh "clients" in the jury box, a dozen men and women picked up the night before and funneled directly into Courtroom 2-11. The people in the gallery seats, most of them already in treatment, have all heard the judge's rap, but for the benefit of the neophytes the judge jumps into it again: "Two options will be given to you

AUTHORS' NOTE: The material in this appendix is from Patrick May, "Drug Court Specializes in Second Chances," *Miami Herald*, October 21, 1990, p. 1B. Reprinted with permission of The Miami Herald.

today. You can go to trial. Or, you can go into the program . . . " He tells them they're facing a third-degree felony for either possession or purchase of up to 28 grams. If convicted, they could do a maximum of 2½ years in prison. Treatment runs about a year. Counselors will help them get a job or training if they want it. If they "graduate" after a year, the judge wipes clean all record of their arrest.

Before Drug Court, many first-time drug offenders got off with credit for time served, sometimes just a night in jail. The fact that most now opt for the program tells the judge that clearing their records and getting help for their addiction is too tempting to pass up. Why else, he says, would they choose a program "when all I'm going to do is aggravate them for an entire year."

One guy nods off. Most, though, lean forward in their seats, eyeing the judge. The judge continues: "The main reason this program works is because we use acupuncture. They stick some needles in your ears to calm you down. It eases the craving for drugs." "I don't know how it works," he says, "but it works." Then comes the pitch: "I know with acupuncture we can get you off cocaine in three to five weeks."

10:30 A.M. . . . They come in all ages, all colors. They speak Spanish and Creole. One wears a nice Italian jacket and string tie. One comes in mud-caked construction boots. Some wear beepers, or earrings in places other than their ears. Some are pregnant. Some check stock listings in the paper. Some are so burned out it's a wonder they found their way in here.

The judge thumbs through computer printouts, each with urinalysis results. If there's progress, the whole courtroom "family"—[the judge, assistant public defender, prosecutor, bailiff]—heaps on the praise. If not, things get messier. One by one, they step up before the judge. "Doing super good," says the judge. "You gonna get your GED?" Rachel: "Yes, judge." Judge: "Great. Keep doing what you're doing, lover, and I'll cut you loose Dec. 13." Rachel: "Thank you."

"What kinda work you doing, Mike?" asks the judge, scowling at the computer printout before him. Mike: "Plasterer." Judge: "I want to see some progress. You can't do your job in jail. Stay clean, will ya? That's why I'm giving you a shot." Mike mumbles: "OK." Judge: "See you in a month."

11:10 A.M. The waitress lights up a cigarette in the hallway. She's 51, a full-blooded Cherokee, a crack lover for years. "I wanted to quit and I knew the only way was to get arrested," she says. "I tried Narcotics Anonymous, detox. I'd gone five months clean before, but could never get past that point. When I finally got arrested, I begged the judge to put me in jail for two weeks. He did." She has been in treatment for eight months, 13 days. "When I came out of jail, everyone in there believed in me so much. I believe in myself now. If I ever feel like I'm going to backslide, I call the judge to talk. I have no family, no one to believe in me. But [the judge] believed in me. He saved my life. That whole courtroom saved my life."

11:30 A.M. The guy in the Italian jacket is Richard . . . , 42, a jeweler from the Bronx with a 20-year heroin habit. "I tried methadone. Nothing really worked. Until now. It's not just the drug program. It's something else, the people. I've never seen a system like this. The counselors lay down the law. If you want to stay straight, they'll help you. These people have all been there, and they kicked."

11:40 A.M. Back in the courtroom, the judge is growling. "I can get you off cocaine," he's telling someone. "But I cannot inject brains into you." The judge has little patience for liars. But his reputation for tough love is backed up by action. He'll throw someone in jail in a heartbeat if he even suspects their alibis. He's respectful with everyone else. . . .

John, 33, steps into the hallway. He says he got into coke as a set designer for rock concerts. He quit for a while, but "down in the dumps" over the loss of a lady friend, John drove into [a high crime area] one night to buy crack. The second time, he bought from a Miami cop. "This court," he says, "gave me a chance to keep from getting screwed up the rest of my life." But as John points out, not everyone is a success. "In acupuncture, you see people who just pull the needles out and sit there talking. They don't take it seriously. I'd say there's a boisterous 20 percent who bull____ their way through. It's 'Yes, Mr. Judge. No, Mr. Judge.'"

A county official connected with the program acknowledges that "The true acid test of this program will be how many get re-arrested in the years to come. I'm not jumping up and down for joy because not all the report cards are back in yet."

TUESDAY, 10:15 A.M. Hugh is livid. As assistant public defender in Drug Court since it began in June 1989, he takes a personal interest in each client. So when someone messes up, Hugh lets them know what he thinks. "See that girl in blue in the jury box?" he says. "We found her last year sleeping under an overpass. In six months, we had her working as [an airlines] reservations clerk. Then she disappears on us." "I have to understand why she made this choice again. I am going to make her life hell between now and next week. I have to convince them all that they can make it, and that is the hardest thing of all to do."

Hugh, who looks and talks like Oliver Hardy, is a bigger-than-life character in this court. He is constantly cuddling up to his clients in the jury box, whispering words of encouragement. "On the other hand," he says, now facing the crowded courtroom, "I look out there and I see a lot of success stories." The girl in blue sits in the corner, her skinny arms stretched tight across her chest in an X, leaning back as if she's trying to melt into the chair, as if she's trying to hide from the judge and Hugh. She'll spend the next two weeks in jail for ditching the program. And then she'll be allowed to start over.

11:30 A.M. The judge looks at his jury box. This morning, between the hookers and the punks reeled in from the night's drug stings, an old man sits, utterly out of place. It's as if somebody's grandpa had accidentally wandered into the wrong room. He is 76 years old. He wears a rumpled pair of green pants and a jail-issue shirt made of what looks like coarse yellow paper. The gentleman slowly rises to his feet when his name is called.

The clerk reads the charge aloud: "Possession of cocaine." The man looks a bit senile. He's too spaced out to even be embarrassed by the predicament he has found himself in this morning. The judge asks gently: "Have you got a drug problem?" "Yes," the man says in a soft voice. Judge: "You want some help?" Elderly man: "Yes." Judge: "You got it, tiger."

Appendix B

The Miami
Drug Court Evaluation

Goldkamp and Weiland (1993a, 1993b), who evaluated the Miami drug court, describe it as a model best perceived as two interrelated components: officials in the courtroom using a judge-directed "team approach" to divert selected defendants to a specially adapted dedicated outpatient drug abuse treatment program (DATP). This model attempts to integrate disparate elements, blending two perspectives that commonly use different methods and that sometimes have contrasting aims in response to individuals' drug involvement. For example, drug treatment programs are accustomed to having the authority to terminate clients' participation based on program-defined criteria. However, in the Miami drug court (MDC) model, the judge decides whether a defendant should be terminated and who, in practice, sends defendants back to treatment without the prior approval of the treatment staff. This hybrid drug court perspective "raises a particular challenge for evaluation research and complicates design of an empirical assessment" (Goldkamp, 1994, p. 117).

Goldkamp and Weiland chose an evaluation design that employed non-equivalent comparison groups of relevant felony defendants (including contemporaneous and historically antecedent samples of noneligible felony drug cases and nondrug cases). They explain that practical issues (an existing 2-year court operational history and unacceptable program disruption from random allocation of defendants to treatment and experimental groups) precluded the use of an experimental design to study the impact of the MDC. The principal sample was a cohort of 326 defendants admitted to the MDC program in August-September 1990. This period was chosen so that the examined defendants were participants in a program that was out of its implementation "infancy." Further, this choice allowed a follow-up period of 18 months from the point of admission to the program for study of defendant behaviors.

Defining the Target Population

A major program design step for the MDC, and a major policy decision, involved defining the initial target population. This process involved carefully balancing the desire to use resources well by targeting a sufficiently challenging group of defendants with concerns that public safety not be jeopardized. For example, if only misdemeanant possession offenders were targeted, case volume could easily have overwhelmed program resources without addressing the issues of criminal caseload processing and jail overcrowding. MDC officials chose as initial eligibility criteria that defendants must be charged with third-degree felony drug possession offenses and must have no prior convictions. They reasoned that such defendants were felons who possibly could be diverted from more extensive case processing and jail, who posed no serious risks to public safety, and for whom intervention payoffs were the likeliest.[1]

"Net widening" is an issue that has been raised in the context of drug courts since their inception. The concern is that, by targeting categories of offenders not usually fully processed by the criminal courts, drug courts might unwittingly add to court workloads and jail populations as well as intervene when intervention is not necessary. By setting sights too low, a drug court may allow to "seep" into its "net" persons who ordinarily would not require many or any of its scarce resources (Goldkamp & Weiland, 1993b, p. 7). Goldkamp and Weiland "found no evidence that the Miami Drug Court noticeably widened the net," although they note that some MDC defendants self-reported that they engaged in no or very minor levels of drug abuse and others tested negatively for drugs upon entering the treatment program. If these self-reports were valid, "the possibility that some in the treatment program did not appear to have serious drug abuse problems raises important questions about targeting and screening procedures." As the investigators also note, the fact that MDC defendants "had their criminal charges dropped or dismissed much less frequently than other types of felony defendants raises the possibility that some would not have ventured very far into criminal processing had they been processed in other criminal courts or during an earlier period." They caution that "the possibility of net widening as an inadvertent side effect should be kept in mind by the Dade County program itself and by other jurisdictions considering similar efforts" (Goldkamp & Weiland, 1993b, p. 7).

Identifying Defendants in the Targeted Population

A rigorous screening mechanism that identifies persons eligible for the program at the earliest stages of processing is a critical element in the MDC model. Underinclusion ("misses") and overinclusion (carelessly including individuals who do not meet the eligibility criteria) are both to be avoided (Goldkamp & Weiland, 1993b, pp. 7-8). The evaluators note that the earliest possible classification of defendants, based on estimated drug involvement and risk to public safety, is needed so that appropriate candidates for drug court diversion can be selected and so that planning can take place for their treatment and community supervision. They observe that a key in such processes in the MDC model "may be closer coordination and computer information exchange between Pretrial Services (or other early processing agency) at the post-arrest interview stage and treatment intake staff. A combination of carefully structured self-report questions about drug use at the Pretrial Services and treatment intake stages and selective initial drug testing, for example, may contribute to improved targeting and programming of MDC candidates" (Goldkamp & Weiland, 1993b, p. 8).

The evaluators devote considerable attention to issues involved in reaching the target population and documenting transactions. Their evaluation was made more difficult by the fact that almost one in three (31%) of all felony defendants charged during August-September 1990 who were assigned to the MDC appeared not to be admitted by the DATP immediately, which raises questions about why some eligible/assigned defendants were missed or did not participate in the voluntary DATP once identified. Goldkamp and Weiland identify several possible reasons for such misses: defendants reconsidered, deciding to decline, preferring to take their chances with regular courts; defendants were able to post bond after initial assignment to MDC, but before the court next convened, and then chose not to participate; Pretrial Services staff missed identifying and interviewing eligible defendants; or defendants agreed to enter DATP, but were no-shows for their first appointments after they were given pretrial release.

The investigators conducted a "careful empirical examination" and determined that "as many as 40 of the 83" defendants in the group thought to have been missed may have entered the DATP through the MDC at some time during the 18-month observation period, just not in the August-September sample period. Goldkamp and Weiland estimate that the miss rate ultimately may have been as small as 17%. These findings suggest that, in fact, the MDC may have had a fairly effective reach (Goldkamp & Weiland, 1993b, p. 10).

Defining and Measuring
Treatment Program Success

Goldkamp and Weiland's evaluation of the MDC hinged on decisions concerning how to define *success* and how to specify definitions of *favorable* and *unfavorable* outcomes. They emphasize that these decisions are matters of policy "to be resolved by debate and consensus among key officials." They recommend that policies that define outcomes "clearly detail the behaviors of participants that are acceptable, that are tolerated but sanctioned in some specified fashion, or that somehow cross the boundary into unacceptable, program-terminating actions." They further advise that the implications of policy enforcement be analyzed in advance of implementation, with periodic review and modification, if necessary, on the basis of program experience (Goldkamp & Weiland, 1993b, p. 8).

Judging from comments made in Goldkamp and Weiland's report, it is obvious that such a debate and consensus had not occurred among the MDC/DATP officials or with the evaluators prior to conduct of the study. The investigators note that measurement of drug program outcomes is "a problem because there are a number of ways to measure 'success,' all of which could be valid depending on the perspective adopted. For purposes of this study, program outcomes were defined as 'favorable' or 'unfavorable' after discussion and debate by members of the judicial working group guiding the research process." This approach was "critical to the assessment so that the research could avoid making policy assumptions that may not have been intended by site officials."

The DATP was initially designed to require defendant progress through three flexibly defined but fairly standard phases to completion (a favorable outcome) in about 12 months. The evaluators cataloged program outcomes by reviewing both the treatment agency files and court-maintained criminal justice data. The specific program outcomes recorded for the sample group at the end of the 18-month (posttreatment entry) observation period included the following types: *unfavorable* (dropped out, terminated); *cases still active* (with no bench warrants; with *alias capiases*); *transferred* (other jurisdiction; other local agency); *other* (deceased); *charges dropped* (within 35 days); *graduation implied* (*nolle prossed*); *nolle prossed,* tracking; sealed; sealed, tracking (probation only). When program outcomes for the 326 defendants who entered DATP immediately after assignment by the MDC were grouped into three categories, 34% were classified as having clearly "favorable" outcomes, 23% were reported to have clearly "unfavorable" outcomes, and the 43% whose classifications were not self-evident fell into the other categories (Goldkamp & Weiland, 1993b, p. 4).

The evaluators also present a "version 2" analysis with redefined favorable and unfavorable outcome measurements to illustrate the role of policy assumptions in the measurement of success. In Version 2 of the outcome analysis, they redefine some outcomes and eliminate 81 cases for the following reasons and assumptions: Transfers to other jurisdictions are null cases; active or open cases at 18 months either were counted provisionally as favorable outcomes (if they did not record *alias capiases*) or were counted provisionally as unfavorable outcomes (if they absconded from the program and did not return to active participation); cases in which charges were dropped within 35 days were excluded from further consideration "because they did not participate in the program for a meaningful period of time (i.e., they were 'false starts')"; cases in which participants dropped out within the first 3 weeks of admission (not just those with charges dropped) were excluded from the analysis "because some minimum period of participation should be required before it is reasonable to evaluate the impact of the program on defendant behavior. . . . This is tantamount to arguing that it is inappropriate to evaluate the impact of an antibiotic if the patient does not take the medication for a sufficient period as prescribed." With the eliminated cases and redefinitions, of the 245 "relevant" defendants, 60% had favorable and 40% had unfavorable outcomes (Goldkamp & Weiland, 1993b, p. 4).

Use of Short-Term Pretrial Detention to Support Program Participation: Motivational Jail

Soon after initiation of the MDC/DATP operations, judicial authorities agreed that something more than reminders, warnings, and threats were needed to convince some program participants that their failure to abide by rules would have real and unpleasant consequences. "The use of a 2-week period of pretrial confinement was intended to provide an option between dismissing a defendant from the program (to face adjudication under normal procedures) and allowing him/her to flounder disastrously on the streets." With attention to concerns that short-term jailing would be overused, a limited number of beds were set aside in Dade County correctional facilities for these purposes. "According to statistics assembled by the office of the State Attorney as of February 24, 1992, 2,245 defendants or approximately 37% of defendants entering the drug court program since its inception had experienced some motivational jail." This equated to an average of approximately 70 per month during this formative 32-month period of the MDC's existence. Some (18%) of the DATP clients had required only one dose of motivation, but 5% were jailed twice and another 5% three or more times (Goldkamp, 1994, pp. 125-126). Information obtained from this same office approximately 18 months later indicated that 62% of the offenders admitted to the program had spent some time in jail for violating program rules—mainly missing scheduled sessions, but also for committing other crimes while enrolled—and 80% of the 62% (or approximately one-half of all enrollees) have had to be remanded to jail twice (K. F. Rundle, personal communication, July 13, 1993).

Restarts and Long-Termers

As indicated by the information already presented, the originally planned smoothly progressing three-phase, 1-year program was not the norm in the MDC/DATP. Nearly one-third started over in Phase I at least once, and about one-third of the program participants were continuing in the program after a 1-year period (Goldkamp, 1994, p. 125). In fact, 28% were reported to have "cases still active" (though not necessarily as a result of being actively enrolled in treatment) at the 18-month point postenrollment (Goldkamp & Weiland, 1993b, p. 4).

Measuring Criminal Justice Outcomes

Caseload outcomes. The evaluators estimated the impact of the MDC on caseload by contrasting the outcomes of drug court defendants with those recorded by other types of felony defendants in samples selected from 1987 and 1990. As expected and as observed in case processing drug courts elsewhere, drug court participants had diversion types of outcomes (*nolle prossed,* case sealed, diverted) recorded more frequently than did other defendants.

Time to completion. Also as predicted, drug court cases took longer to complete; nearly a third of MDC cases were still open (unadjudicated) at the end of the 18-month observation period, in contrast to virtually no open cases among comparison groups. The evaluators attribute this discrepancy to DATP clients who are required to stay in the DATP for much longer than was originally planned and the practice of leaving the cases of DATP clients who abscond in active status indefinitely. As Goldkamp (1994) notes, "It is impossible to determine with certainty whether the longer completion time contributes to greater use of court resources than normal criminal processing does" (p. 124).

Dismissals and sentence lengths. Two other findings of particular interest to criminal justice authorities are as follows: (a) Greater proportions of cases in the 1990 and 1987 comparison samples were dropped or dismissed (including "no action"), and (b) far fewer MDC defendants were sentenced to terms of incarceration of more than 1 year than were other felony drug and nondrug defendants being processed contemporaneously (Goldkamp, 1994, p. 125). The first finding raises the issue of net widening mentioned earlier. The second might suggest a greater "leniency" in the drug court, a perception that drug court officials hope to avoid and one that can create tremendous public relations problems for them.

Failures to appear. As could have been predicted, as an artifact of requiring multiple court hearings (for scheduled progress reports and ad hoc motivational sessions) during defendants' enrollment in the DATP, program participants had a high failure-to-appear (FTA) rate. More than half of the MDC defendants recorded FTAs, compared with 2-11% of other felony defendant samples. The evaluators note that this is usual for such programs, but that procedures can be devised to monitor appearances more closely to reduce FTAs (Goldkamp, 1994, p. 128).

Rearrests. MDC defendants were found to generate somewhat lower rates of rearrest than the comparison sample of 1990 nondrug felony defendants. They accounted for notably lower rates of rearrest than other second- and third-degree felony drug defendants processed through other local courtrooms. When compared with the sample of 1987 felony drug defendants, the MDC defendant sample reflected much lower rates of rearrest, even after the researchers controlled for possible differences in sample composition (Goldkamp & Weiland, 1993b, p. 5).

Time to rearrest. When MDC defendants were rearrested, the lapsed time to their first rearrests averaged from two to three times longer than those of defendants in comparison felony samples (Goldkamp & Weiland, 1993b, p. 5).

Other System Issues

Need for different treatment programs. Goldkamp and Weiland (1993b) note that a critical element of the MDC was the development of a dedicated custom-designed outpatient substance abuse treatment program. They accurately state that the program made provisions for residential placements for a very limited number of individuals (p. 7) and imply that the MDC/DATP should give more attention to the concept of "client-treatment matching":

In differentiating entering defendants according to estimated drug-involvement and public safety risk, an improved initial stage classification approach can help target Drug Court defendants efficiently to treatment regimens of possibly different substance and length, while still ensuring equitable treatment of defendants overall.

Such a classification could maximize efficient use of resources by assigning lower-risk and less drug-involved defendants to somewhat shorter programs of treatment to be complemented by other non-incarcerative options while channeling medium-risk and more seriously drug-involved defendants into longer and more intensive programs. For equity, an aim would be to provide equivalent diversionary programs so that defendants are treated similarly overall, even given their different content. (Goldkamp & Weiland, 1993b, p. 8)

Impact of the MDC on the jurisdiction's criminal caseload. Given that one of the objectives of most drug courts is to reduce the stress placed on criminal courtrooms by drug cases, it is instructive to note some of the caseload statistics reported by the evaluators. They estimate that 39% of all entering second- and third-degree felony cases in this jurisdiction involved drug offenses and report that about 13% of these cases were identified as eligible and scheduled for MDC processing. Given carryover from previous months' filings, the evaluators report that the MDC processed the equivalent of 5-7% of all entering second- and third-degree felony cases in its jurisdiction (Goldkamp, 1994, p. 126).

Resource implications of the drug court program. Obviously, the "cost-effectiveness" of the drug treatment court approach is a legitimate interest of court systems administrators, budget analysts, and elected government officials alike. Goldkamp and Weiland's assessment of the MDC was not designed as a cost-effectiveness study, but cost considerations are critical to an overall appraisal of the promise of the MDC or similar drug court models. Cost-efficiency (cost-effectiveness and cost-benefits) analyses are complex and difficult, and outcomes are heavily dependent on a variety of costs and savings assumptions. Principal foci for analyses must consider the costs associated with (a) dedicated drug case courtroom operations, (b) treatment costs, and (c) the costs of missed appearances and program misstarts, as well as possible savings in (d) case processing, (e) confinement, and (f) reduced or slowed rates of reoffending (Goldkamp & Weiland, 1993b, p. 8).

Evaluation perspectives. Evaluation researchers have both an opportunity and a responsibility to promote evaluations of treatment-oriented drug courts that encompass the goals and performance of the other "subsystems" involved, such as law enforcement, prosecution, public health, and general social services, as well as substance abuse treatment. As Mahoney (1994) notes, "Perhaps even more important, we need to learn about the extent to which truly integrated program planning and implementation takes place, cutting across all the subsystems including the courts, and find out what it takes to achieve effective integrated planning and operations" (p. 131).

Note

1. Goldkamp and Weiland (1993b) note in their initial report that "assessment findings suggest that the criteria for eligibility might be broadened to include other types of drug-involved felony-level defendants who may not be charged with drug offenses." Indeed, the researchers include in that report the statement, "By 1990, persons with initial charges involving selected second-degree drug felonies (purchase

of drugs) were considered for the program as well as some defendants with prior convictions" (p. 11). In a later journal article, Goldkamp (1994) states, "It is difficult to determine how this broadening of the eligibility criteria may have occurred." After speculating about the various ways it could have happened and the implications for caseload, he notes, "The assessment findings provide an opportunity to review the implications of the drug court's targeting approach and to consider what other categories of felony defendants, if any, could be safely and effectively targeted for the drug court approach" (p. 148). His subsequent analyses present a risk-assessment scheme that he suggests might identify appropriate drug court participants from pools of defendants with more serious immediate charges and/or criminal justice histories. As discussed briefly above, movement in such a direction has attendant political and public relations risks.

References

Adams, S., & McArthur, V. (1969). *Performance of narcotics-involved prison releasees under three kinds of community experience* (Research Report No. 16). Washington: District of Columbia Department of Corrections.

Adler, J. (1988, November 28). Crack: Hour by hour, the plague feeds on junkies and cops, hookers and babies—and all of us. *Newsweek, 112,* 64.

Advice for the new drug czar. (1991, February 15). *Miami Herald,* p. 32.

Agar, M. (1973). *Ripping and running: A formal ethnography of heroin addicts.* New York: Seminar.

American Bar Association Commission on Correctional Facilities Services. (1975). *Pre-trial criminal justice intervention technique and action programs.* Chicago: Author.

Anderson, N. (1923). *The hobo: The sociology of the homeless man.* Chicago: University of Chicago Press.

Anglin, M. D. (1988). The efficacy of civil commitment in treating narcotic addiction. In C. G. Leukefeld & F. M. Tims (Eds.), *Compulsory treatment of drug abuse: Research and clinical practice* (Research Monograph 86) (pp. 8-34). Washington, DC: U.S. Department of Health and Human Services.

Anslinger, H. J. (1951, April-June). Relationship between addiction to narcotic drugs and crime. *Bulletin on Narcotics.*

Anslinger, H. J., & Tompkins, W. F. (1953). *The traffic in narcotics.* New York: Funk & Wagnalls.

Ashbury, H. (1933). *The Barbary Coast.* Garden City, NY: Garden City.

Austin, G. A., & Lettieri, D. J. (1976). *Drugs and crime: The relationship of drug use and concomitant criminal behavior.* Rockville, MD: National Institute on Drug Abuse.

Bailey, W. C. (1956). Individual counseling and group psychotherapy with paroled drug addicts: A pilot field experiment. *Research Studies, State College of Washington, 24,* 141-149.

Ball, J. C., & Chambers, C. D. (1970). *The epidemiology of opiate addiction in the United States.* Springfield, IL: Charles C Thomas.

Ball, J. C., & Lau, M. P. (1966). The Chinese narcotic addict in the United States. *Social Forces, 45*(1).

Ball, J. C., Shaffer, J. W., & Nurco, D. N. (1983). The day-to-day criminality of heroin addicts in Baltimore: A study in the continuity of offense rates. *Drug and Alcohol Dependence, 12,* 119-142.

Bayer, R. (1991). Introduction: The great drug policy debate—What means this thing called decriminalization? *Milbank Quarterly, 69,* 341-363.

Becker, H. S. (1963). *Outsiders.* New York: Free Press.

Belenko, S. (1990). The impact of drug offenders on the criminal justice system. In R. A. Weisheit (Ed.), *Drugs, crime, and the criminal justice system.* Cincinnati, OH: Anderson.

Belenko, S., Davis, R. C., & Dumanovsky, T. (1992). *Drug felony case processing in New York City's N Parts: Interim report to Bureau of Justice Assistance, U.S. Department of Justice.* New York: New York City Criminal Justice Agency.

Belenko, S., & Dumanovsky, T. (1993). *Special drug courts: Program brief.* Washington, DC: U.S. Department of Justice, Bureau of Justice Assistance, Office of Justice Programs.

Belenko, S., Fagan, J., & Chin, K. (1991). Criminal justice responses to crack. *Journal of Research in Crime and Delinquency, 28*(1).

Belenko, S., Fagan, J., & Dumanovsky, T. (1994). The effects of legal sanctions on recidivism in special drug courts. In Swift and effective justice: New approaches to drug cases in the states [Special issue]. *Justice System Journal, 17,* 53-81.

Bennett, W. J. (1990). Drug policy and the intellectuals. *International Journal on Drug Policy, 1*(6), 16-18.

Bennett, W. J., Jackson, J., & Schmoke, K. L. (1989). Moralism and realism in the drug war. *New Perspectives Quarterly, 6*(2).

Black, J. (1927). *You can't win.* New York: Macmillan.

Board of Trustees. (1990). Legal interventions during pregnancy: Court-ordered medical treatments and legal penalties for potentially harmful behavior by pregnant women. *Journal of the American Medical Association, 264,* 2663-2670.

Braude, J. M. (1948). Boys' court: Individualized justice for the youthful offender. *Federal Probation, 12,* 9-14.

Brill, L., & Lieberman, L. (1970). *Authority and addiction.* Boston: Little, Brown.

Brown, J. W., Mazze, R., & Glaser, D. (1974). *Narcotics knowledge and nonsense: Program disaster versus a scientific model.* Cambridge, MA: Ballinger.

Buckley, W. F., Jr. (1988, October 28). Koppel's drug bust [in On the right]. *National Review, 40,* 63.

Buckley, W. F., Jr. (1989, September 29). A lost cause is a lost cause [in On the right]. *National Review, 41,* 70-71.

Buel, J. W. (1891). *Sunlight and shadow of America's great cities.* Philadelphia: West Philadelphia.

Byrnes, T. (1886). *Professional criminals of America*. New York: G. W. Dillingham.

Byrnes, T. (1895). *Professional criminals of America* (2nd ed.). New York: G. W. Dillingham.

Campbell, H., Knox, T. W., & Byrnes, T. (1892). *Darkness and daylight; Or, lights and shadows of New York life*. Hartford, CT: A. D. Worthington.

Carver, J. A. (1986, September-October). Drugs and crime: Controlling use and reducing risk through testing. *NIJ Reports*.

Casey, P. (1994). Court-enforced drug treatment programs: Do they enhance court performance? In Swift and effective justice: New approaches to drug cases in the states [Special issue]. *Justice System Journal, 17*, 117-126.

Castro, K. G., Lieb, S., Jaffe, H. W., Narkunas, J. P., Calisher, C., Bush, T., & Witte, J. J. (1988). Transmission of HIV in Belle Glade, Florida: Lessons for other communities in the United States. *Science, 239*, 193-197.

Chaisson, R. E., Moss, A. R., Onishi, R., Osmond, D., & Carlson, J. R. (1987). Human immunodeficiency virus infection in heterosexual intravenous drug users in San Francisco. *American Journal of Public Health, 77*, 169-172.

Chambers, C. D., Cuskey, W. R., & Moffett, A. D. (1970). Demographic factors in opiate addiction among Mexican-Americans. *Public Health Reports, 85*, 523-531.

Chein, I. (1966, February). Psychological, social, and epidemiological factors in drug addiction. In *Rehabilitating the narcotic addict* (report of the Institute on New Developments in Rehabilitating the Narcotic Addict). Washington, DC: Government Printing Office.

Church, T., Carlson, A., Lee, J. L., & Tan, T. (1978). *Justice delayed: The pace of litigation in urban trial courts*. Williamsburg, VA: National Center for State Courts.

Clayton, R. R. (1989). Legalization of drugs: An idea whose time has not come. *American Behavioral Scientist, 32*(3).

Clemmer, D. M. (1950). On imprisonment as a source of criminality. *Journal of Criminal Law, Criminology and Police Science, 41*, 311-319.

Clemmer, D. M. (1958). *The prison community*. New York: Rinehart.

Collins, J. J., & Allison, M. (1983). Legal coercion and retention in drug abuse treatment. *Hospital and Community Psychiatry, 34*, 1145-1149.

Collins, J. J., Hubbard, R. L., Raschal, J. V., Cavanaugh, E. R., & Craddock, S. G. (1982a). *Client characteristics, behaviors and intreatment outcomes: 1980 TOPS admission cohort*. Research Triangle Park, NC: Research Triangle Institute.

Collins, J. J., Hubbard, R. L., Raschal, J. V., Cavanaugh, E. R., & Craddock, S. G. (1982b). *Criminal justice clients in drug treatment*. Research Triangle Park, NC: Research Triangle Institute.

Collins, S. (1887). *The habitual use of narcotic poison*. LaPorte, IN: Theriaki.

Cooper, C. S., Soloman, M., Bakke, H., & Lane, T. (1991). *BJA pilot Expedited Drug Case Management (EDCM) program: Overview and program summaries*. Washington, DC: American University.

Cooper, C. S., & Trotter, J. A., Jr. (1994). Recent developments in drug case management: Re-engineering the judicial process. In Swift and effective justice: New approaches to drug cases in the states [Special issue]. *Justice System Journal, 17*, 83-98.

Corn, D., Gravley, E., & Morley, J. (1989, February). Drug czars we have known. *The Nation*, p. 258.

Costello, A. E. (1885). *Our police protectors*. New York: Author.

Council for Science and Society. (1981). *Treating the troublesome: The ethical problems of compulsory medical treatment for socially unacceptable behaviour.* London: Author.

Courtwright, D. T. (1982). *Dark paradise: Opiate addiction in America before 1940.* Cambridge, MA: Harvard University Press.

Covington, J. (1987). Addict attitudes toward legalization of heroin. *Contemporary Drug Problems, 14,* 315-353.

Cowan, R. C. (1986, December 5). How the narcs created crack: A war against ourselves. *National Review, 38,* 26-28.

Crapsey, E. (1872). *The nether side of New York.* New York: Sheldon.

Cronin, T. E., Cronin, T. Z., & Milakovich, M. E. (1981). *U.S. v. crime in the streets.* Bloomington: Indiana University Press.

Dai, B. (1937). *Opium addiction in Chicago.* Shanghai: Commercial.

Davis, R. C., Smith, B. E., & Lurigio, A. J. (1994). Court strategies to cope with rising drug caseloads. In Swift and effective justice: New approaches to drug cases in the states [Special issue]. *Justice System Journal, 17,* 1-18.

Decriminalizing drugs? The U.S. surgeon-general has revived a long-simmering debate about existing legal restraints on drug abuse. (1993, December). *Nature, 366,* 598.

Defense demurs: Hoots for a drug plan. (1986, September 29). *Time,* p. 36.

DeFleur, L. B., Ball, J. C., & Snarr, R. W. (1969, Fall). The long-term social correlates of opiate addiction. *Social Problems, 16.*

DeLoughry, T. J. (1989). Bennett asks for an end to federal aid to colleges that fail to punish students for illegal drug use. *Chronicle of Higher Education, 35*(49).

Des Jarlais, D. C., Wish, E., Friedman, S. R., Stoneburner, R., Yancovitz, S. R., Milsvan, D., El-Sadr, W., Brady, E., & Cudrado, M. (1987). Intravenous drug use and the heterosexual transmission of the human immunodeficiency virus: Current trends in New York City. *New York State Journal of Medicine, 87,* 283-286.

Diskind, M. H., & Klonsky, G. (1964a). *Recent developments in the treatment of paroled offenders addicted to narcotic drugs.* Albany: New York State Division of Parole.

Diskind, M. H., & Klonsky, G. (1964b). A second look at the New York State Parole Drug Experiment. *Federal Probation, 28,* 34-41.

Dole, V. P. (1972). Detoxification of sick addicts in prison. *Journal of the American Medical Association, 220,* 366-369.

Dole, V. P., Robinson, J. W., Orraca, J., Towns, E., Searcy, P., & Caine, E. (1969). Methadone treatment of randomly selected criminal addicts. *New England Journal of Medicine, 280,* 1372-1375.

Dombrink, J., & Meeker, J. W. (1986). Beyond "buy and bust": Nontraditional sanctions in federal drug law enforcement. *Contemporary Drug Problems, 13,* 711-740.

Dugdale, R. L. (1877). *The Jukes: A study in crime, pauperism, disease and heredity.* New York: G. P. Putnam's Sons.

Dwyer, J. (1971). Volunteers help prisoner addicts. *Rehabilitation Record, 12,* 12-14.

Eckerman, W. C., Bates, J. K., Raschal, J. V., & Poole, W. K. (1976). Insights into the relationship between drug usage and crime derived from a study of arrestees. In Research Triangle Institute, *Appendix to drug use and crime: Report of the Panel on Drug Use and Criminal Behavior* (pp. 387-407). Research Triangle Park, NC: Research Triangle Institute.

Epstein, E. J. (1977). *Agency of fear.* New York: Putnam.

Evicting the drug dealers: Kemp's tough action raises constitutional questions. (1989, May 1). *Time, 113,* 41.

Faris, R. E. L., & Dunham, H. W. (1939). *Mental disorders in urban areas*. Chicago: University of Chicago Press.

Farkas, G. M., Petersen, D. M., & Barr, N. I. (1970). New developments in the Federal Bureau of Prisons Addict Treatment Program. *Federal Probation, 34,* 52-59.

Faupel, C. E. (1991). *Shooting dope: Career patterns of hard-core heroin users*. Gainesville: University of Florida Press.

Finn, P., & Newlyn, A. K. (1993a, November). Miami drug court gives drug defendants a second chance. *National Institute of Justice Journal: Research in Action,* pp. 13-20.

Finn, P., & Newlyn, A. K. (1993b). *Miami's "drug court": A different approach* (Program Focus, NCJ 142412). Washington, DC: U.S. Department of Justice, National Institute of Justice, Office of Justice Programs.

Flicker, B. (1990, February). To jail or not to jail? *ABA Journal, 76.*

Ford, A., Hauser, H., & Jackson, E., Jr. (1975). Use of drugs among persons admitted to a county jail. *Public Health Reports, 90,* 504-508.

Gandossy, R. P., Williams, J. R., Cohen, J., & Harwood, H. J. (1980). *Drugs and crime: A survey and analysis of the literature*. Washington, DC: U.S. Department of Justice.

Geelhoed, G. W. (1984). The addict's angioaccess: Complications of exotic vascular injection sites. *New York State Journal of Medicine, 84,* 585-586.

Gest, T. (1989, February 6). The pregnancy police, on patrol: Authorities are charging women who endanger their fetuses. *U.S. News & World Report, 106,* 50.

Gest, T. (1990, April 9). Little hope for justice: Why the latest fix-it plan is unlikely to ease the courts' crisis. *U.S. News & World Report, 108,* 24-27.

Gibbons, D. C. (1965). *Changing the lawbreaker: The treatment of delinquents and criminals*. Englewood Cliffs, NJ: Prentice Hall.

Gitlin, T. (1987). *The sixties: Years of hope, years of rage*. New York: Bantam.

Glaser, D., Inciardi, J. A., & Babst, D. V. (1969). Later heroin use by marijuana-using, heroin-using, and non-drug-using adolescent offenders in New York City. *International Journal of the Addictions, 4,* 145-155.

Goldkamp, J. S. (1994). Miami's treatment drug court for felony defendants: Some implications of assessment findings. *Prison Journal, 73,* 110-166.

Goldkamp, J. S., & Weiland, D. (1993a). *Assessing the impact of Dade County's felony drug court* (Research Report No. NCJ 144524). Washington, DC: U.S. Department of Justice, National Institute of Justice, Office of Justice Programs.

Goldkamp, J. S., & Weiland, D. (1993b, December). Assessing the impact of Dade County's felony drug court. *Research in Brief Evaluation Bulletin.*

Goldkamp, J. S., & Weiland, D. (1993c). *Assessing the impact of Dade County's felony drug court: Executive summary*. Philadelphia: Crime and Justice Research Institute.

Goldstein, A., & Kalant, H. (1990, September). Drug policy: Striking the right balance. *Science, 249.*

Goldstein, P. J. (1979). *Prostitution and drugs*. Lexington, MA: Lexington.

Greenberg, S. W., & Adler, F. (1974). Crime and addiction: An empirical analysis of the literature, 1920-1973. *Contemporary Drug Problems, 3,* 221-270.

Hackett, G. (1989, May 29). On the firing line: Outmanned and outgunned, police are feeling the stress of the drug war. *Newsweek, 113,* 32-34, 36.

Hansen, M. (1992, November). Courts side with moms in drug cases: Florida woman's conviction overturned for delivering cocaine via umbilical cord. *ABA Journal, 78.*

Hapgood, H. (1903). *The autobiography of a thief.* New York: Fox, Duffield.

Hobson, R. P. (1928). The struggle of mankind against its deadliest foe. *Narcotic Education, 1,* 51-54.

Hubbard, R. L., Collins, J. J., Raschal, J. V., & Cavanaugh, E. R. (1988). The criminal justice client in drug abuse treatment. In C. G. Leukefeld & F. M. Tims (Eds.), *Compulsory treatment of drug abuse: Research and clinical practice* (pp. 57-80). Rockville, MD: National Institute on Drug Abuse.

Hubbard, R. L., Marsden, M. E., Raschal, J. V., Harwood, H. J., Cavanaugh, E. R., & Ginzburg, H. M. (1989). *Drug abuse treatment: A national study of effectiveness.* Chapel Hill: University of North Carolina Press.

Illinois Institute for Juvenile Research & the Chicago Area Project. (1953). *Report of the Chicago narcotics survey.* Unpublished manuscript.

Inciardi, J. A. (1974). The vilification of euphoria: Some perspectives on an elusive issue. *Addictive Diseases: An International Journal, 1,* 241-267.

Inciardi, J. A. (1975). *Careers in crime.* Chicago: Rand McNally.

Inciardi, J. A. (1979). Heroin use and street crime. *Crime & Delinquency, 25,* 335-346.

Inciardi, J. A. (1986). *The war on drugs: Heroin, cocaine, crime, and public policy.* Palo Alto, CA: Mayfield.

Inciardi, J. A. (1988). Compulsory treatment in New York: A brief narrative history of misjudgment, mismanagement, and misrepresentation. *Journal of Drug Issues, 18,* 547-560.

Inciardi, J. A. (Ed.). (1991). *The drug legalization debate.* Newbury Park, CA: Sage.

Inciardi, J. A. (1992a). The great drug war and the great drug debate: Wrangling over control versus legalization. In J. A. Inciardi (Ed.), *The war on drugs II: The continuing epic of heroin, cocaine, crack, crime, AIDS, and public policy* (pp. 233-259). Mountain View, CA: Mayfield.

Inciardi, J. A. (Ed.). (1992b). *The war on drugs II: The continuing epic of heroin, cocaine, crack, crime, AIDS, and public policy.* Mountain View, CA: Mayfield.

Inciardi, J. A., & Chambers, C. D. (1972). Unreported criminal involvement of narcotic addicts. *Journal of Drug Issues, 2,* 57-64.

Inciardi, J. A., Lockwood, D., & Pottieger, A. E. (1993). *Women and crack-cocaine.* New York: Macmillan.

Inciardi, J. A., & Pottieger, A. E. (1986). Drug use and crime among two cohorts of women narcotics users: An empirical assessment. *Journal of Drug Issues, 16,* 91-106.

Irwin, W. (1909). *The confessions of a con man.* New York: B. W. Huebsch.

Jacoby, J. E. (1994). Expedited drug case management programs: Some lessons in case management reform. In Swift and effective justice: New approaches to drug cases in the states [Special issue]. *Justice System Journal, 17,* 19-40.

Jacoby, J. E., Ratledge, E. C., & Gramckow, H. P. (1992). *Expedited drug case management program: Issues and implications for program development, final report.* Washington, DC: U.S. Department of Justice, National Institute of Justice.

James, J. (1976). Prostitution and addiction. *Addictive Diseases: An International Journal, 2,* 601-618.

Jaschik, S. (1989). Investigators to visit campuses to check for illegal drug use; Probe will focus on compliance with law by Pell Grant recipients. *Chronicle of Higher Education, 35*(1).

Jefferson Institute for Justice Studies. (1992). *An evaluation of the Expedited Drug Case Management program 42.* Washington, DC: Author.

Johnson, B. D., et al. (1985). *Taking care of business: The economics of crime by heroin users.* Lexington, MA: Lexington.

Joint Committee on New York Drug Law Evaluation. (1977). *The nation's toughest drug law: Evaluation of the New York experience.* New York: Association of the Bar of the City of New York.

Joseph, H., & Dole, V. P. (1970). Methadone patients on probation and parole. *Federal Probation, 34,* 42-48.

Kane, J. P. (1992). The challenge of legalizing drugs. *America, 167*(3), 61-63.

King, R. (1972). *The drug hang-up: America's fifty year folly.* New York: W. W. Norton.

King, R. (1974). The American system: Legal sanctions to repress drug abuse. In J. A. Inciardi & C. D. Chambers (Eds.), *Drugs and the criminal justice system* (pp. 17-37). Beverly Hills, CA: Sage.

Knox, T. W. (1873). *Underground or life below the surface.* Hartford, CT: J. B. Burr & Hyde.

Kolb, L. (1925, January). Drug addiction and its relation to crime. *Mental Hygiene, 9,* 74-89.

Kolb, L. (1962). *Drug addiction: A medical problem.* Springfield, IL: Charles C Thomas.

Kreiter, M. S. (1987). Fighting drugs; A look at the new laws and changed attitudes. *Current Health, 2*(13).

Law Enforcement Assistance Administration. (1973). *TASC guidelines.* Washington, DC: Author.

Leen, J., & Van Natta, D., Jr. (1994a, August 29). Crime and punishment drug court: Drug court favored by felons. *Miami Herald,* p. 1A.

Leen, J., & Van Natta, D., Jr. (1994b, August 29). Crime and punishment drug court: Is the program working? Who knows? *Miami Herald,* p. 6A.

Leiberg, L. G. (1971). *Project Crossroads: Final report.* Washington, DC: National Committee for Children and Youth.

Lemert, E. M. (1972). *Human deviance, social problems and social control* (2nd ed.). Englewood Cliffs, NJ: Prentice Hall.

Lening, G. (1873). *The dark side of New York life and its criminal classes.* New York: Fred'k Gerhand.

Leukefeld, C. G., & Tims, F. M. (Eds.). (1988). *Compulsory treatment of drug abuse: Research and clinical practice.* Rockville, MD: National Institute on Drug Abuse.

Levine, H. G., & Reinarman, C. (1991). From prohibition to regulation: Lessons from alcohol policy for drug policy. *Milbank Quarterly, 69,* 461-494.

Lichtenstein, P. M. (1914). Narcotic addiction. *New York Medical Journal, 100,* 962-966.

Lindesmith, A. R. (1965). *The addict and the law.* Bloomington: Indiana University Press.

Lipscher, R. D. (1989). The judicial response to the drug crisis: A report of an executive symposium involving judicial leaders of the nation's nine most populous states. *State Court Journal, 13*(4).

Lowinson, J. H., & Jaffe, J. H. (1995). Art of acupuncture. In *Encyclopedia of drugs and alcohol* (Vol. 3, pp. 1141-1144). New York: Simon & Schuster/Macmillan.

Maddux, J. F. (1978). History of the hospital treatment programs, 1935-1974. In W. R. Martin & H. Isbell (Eds.), *Drug addiction and the U.S. public health service* (pp. 217-250). Washington, DC: U.S. Department of Health, Education and Welfare.

Maddux, J. F. (1988). *Clinical experience with civil commitment in compulsory treatment of drug abuse: Research and clinical practice* (NIDA Services Research Monograph Series 86, DHHS Publication No. 88-1578). Washington, DC: Government Printing Office.

Magnuson, E. (1988, March 14). Tears of rage: Americans lose patience with Panama and with a failed drug policy. *Time*, pp. 18-20.

Mahoney, B. (1994). Drug courts: What have we learned so far? In Swift and effective justice: New approaches to drug cases in the states [Special issue]. *Justice System Journal, 17,* 127-133.

Manhattan Court Employment Project. (1972). *Manhattan Court Employment Project: Final report.* New York: Vera Institute of Justice.

Marshall, E. (1988, September). Drug wars: Legalization gets a hearing. *Science, 241.*

Martin, E. W. (1868). *Sins of the great city.* Philadelphia: National.

Marwick, C. (1989). Redeclared war on illegal drugs: Most agree with intent, but how? *Journal of the American Medical Association, 262*(13).

Maurer, D. W. (1964). *Whiz mob: A correlation of the technical argot of pickpockets with their behavior pattern.* New Haven, CT: College University Press.

May, P. (1990, October 21). Drug court specializes in second chances. *Miami Herald,* p. 1B.

McBride, D. C. (1976). The relationship between type of drug use and arrest charge in an arrested population. In Research Triangle Institute, *Appendix to drug use and crime: Report of the Panel on Drug Use and Criminal Behavior* (pp. 409-418). Research Triangle Park, NC: Research Triangle Institute.

McBride, D. C. (1978). Criminal justice diversion. In J. A. Inciardi & K. C. Haas (Eds.), *Crime and the criminal justice process* (pp. 246-259). Dubuque, IA: Kendall/Hunt.

McBride, D. C., & Bennett, A. L. (1978). The impact of criminal justice diversion on a community drug treatment structure. *Drug Forum, 8*(1), 1-10.

McBride, D. C., & McCoy, C. B. (1981). Crime and drug-using behavior: An areal analysis. *Criminology, 19,* 281-302.

McBride, D. C., & McCoy, C. B. (1982). Crime and drugs: The issues and the literature. *Journal of Drug Issues, 12,* 137-152.

McBride, D. C., & McCoy, C. B. (1993). The drugs-crime relationship: An analytical framework. *Prison Journal, 73,* 257-278.

McBride, D. C., & Swartz, J. (1990). Drugs and violence. In R. Weisheit (Ed.), *Drugs, crime and the criminal justice system.* Cincinnati, OH: Anderson.

McGlothlin, W. H., Anglin, M. D., & Wilson, B. D. (1977). *An evaluation of the California civil addict program* (NIDA Services Research Monograph Series, DHEW Publication No. ADM 78-558). Washington, DC: Government Printing Office.

McLaughlin, J. (1989, March 10). Czar without a throne? (Drug czar William Bennett). *National Review, 41,* 19.

Meiselas, H., & Brill, L. (1974). The role of civil commitment in multi-modality programming. In J. A. Inciardi & C. D. Chambers (Eds.), *Drugs and the criminal justice system* (pp. 171-182). Beverly Hills, CA: Sage.

Michelson, T. (1940). Lindesmith's mythology. *Journal of Criminal Law and Criminology, 31,* 375-400.

Middleton, M. (1992). Do drug courts work? Critics say minor cases flood the system. *National Law Journal, 15*(9).

Milkman, R. H., Beaudin, B. D., Tarmann, K., & Landson, N. (1992). *Drug offenders and the courts: A national assessment.* McLean, VA: Lazar Institute.

Milkman, R. H., Beaudin, B. D., Tarmann, K., & Landson, N. (1993). *Drug offenders and the courts: Summary of a national assessment* (Public Policy Paper No. 921). McLean, VA: Lazar Institute.

Miller, M. (1989, April 24). Unveiling Bennett's battle plan: William Bennett to curb drug-related violence in Washington. *Newsweek, 113,* 6.

Moore, M. H. (1991). Drugs, the criminal law, and the administration of justice (Confronting drug policy: Part 2). *Milbank Quarterly, 69*(4).

Morgan, H. W. (1974). *Yesterday's addicts: American society and drug abuse, 1865-1929.* Norman: University of Oklahoma Press.

Morgan, J. P., Jr. (1965, July-August). Drug addiction: Criminal or medical problem. *Police,* pp. 6-9.

Morganthau, T. (1988, March 14). Losing the war? *Newsweek,* pp. 16-18.

Morganthau, T. (1990, April 16). Uncivil liberties? Debating whether drug-war tactics are eroding constitutional rights. *Time, 135,* 18.

Morganthau, T., & Miller, M. (1989, April 10). The drug warrior; Bill Bennett is an ambitious, impatient man with a mission many people think is impossible. Can he overcome the odds and get the job done? The drug crisis. *Newsweek, 113,* 20-24.

Morley, J., & Byrne, M. (1989). The drug war and "national security": The making of a quagmire, 1969-1973. *Dissent, 36*(1).

Musto, D. F. (1973). *The American disease.* New Haven, CT: Yale University Press.

Muth, H. (1902, May). *Drug abuse.* Paper presented at the Ninth Annual Meeting of the International Association of Chiefs of Police.

Nadelmann, E. A. (1988a, Summer). The case for legalization. *Public Interest, 92,* 3.

Nadelmann, E. A. (1988b, June 13). Shooting up: Crime and the drug laws. *New Republic, 198,* 16-17.

Nadelmann, E. A. (1989). Drug prohibition in the United States: Costs, consequences, and alternatives. *Science, 245,* 939-947.

National Highway Traffic Administration. (1985). *Impact of a driver intervention program on DWI recidivism and problem drinking.* Washington, DC: U.S. Department of Transportation.

National Institute of Justice. (1988). *Drug use forecasting.* Washington, DC: Author.

Nellans, C. T., & Massee, J. C. (1928). Management of drug addicts in United States penitentiary at Atlanta. *Journal of the American Medical Association, 92,* 1153-1155.

Newmeyer, J. A. (1987, November). Role of the IV drug user and the secondary spread of AIDS. *Street Pharmacologist, 11,* 1-2.

Nurco, D. N., Ball, J. C., Shaffer, J. W., & Hanlon, T. F. (1985). The criminality of narcotic addicts. *Journal of Nervous and Mental Disease, 173,* 94-102.

O'Donnell, J. A. (1966, Spring). Narcotic addiction and crime. *Social Problems, 13.*

O'Donnell, J. A. (1969). *Narcotic addicts in Kentucky* (DHEW Publication). Washington, DC: Government Printing Office.

Off to war they go: George Bush's war against drugs. (1989, September). *Economist, 312,* 28.

Panacea or chaos? The legalization of drugs in America. (1994). *Journal of Substance Abuse Treatment, 11*(1).

Panel presentation. (1990). *Judicature, 73*(6).

Park, R. E., Burgess, E. W., & MacKenzie, R. D. (1925). *The city.* Chicago: University of Chicago Press.

Pearson, G. (1989). The street connection: Small drug pushers are the key to controlling drugs. *New Statesman and Society, 2*(67).

Perlman, H., & Jaszi, P. (1976). *Legal issues in addict diversion*. Lexington, MA: Lexington.

Pescor, M. J. (1943). A statistical analysis of the clinical records of hospitalized drug addicts. *Public Health Reports, 58*(Suppl. 143).

Petersen, D. M. (1974). Some reflections on compulsory treatment of addiction. In J. A. Inciardi & C. D. Chambers (Eds.), *Drugs and the criminal justice system* (pp. 143-169). Beverly Hills, CA: Sage.

Petersen, D. M., Yarvis, R. M., & Farkas, G. M. (1969). The Federal Bureau of Prisons treatment program for narcotic addicts. *Federal Probation, 33,* 35-40.

Plair, W., & Jackson, L. (1970). *Narcotic use and crime: A report on interviews with 50 addicts under treatment*. Washington, DC: U.S. Department of Corrections.

President's Commission on Law Enforcement and Administration of Justice. (1967). *Task force report: Narcotics and drug abuse*. Washington, DC: Government Printing Office.

Press, A. (1986, September 8). Reality versus rhetoric; How politicians respond to the crack epidemic. *Newsweek, 108,* 60.

Quinn, T. C., Glasser, D., Cannon, R., Matuszak, D. I., Dunning, R. W., Klein, R. L., Campbell, C., Israel, E., Fauci, A., & Hook, E. W. (1988). Human immunodeficiency virus infection among patients attending clinics for sexually transmitted diseases. *New England Journal of Medicine, 318,* 197-203.

Ratner, M. (1993). *Crack pipe as pimp*. Lexington, MA: Lexington.

Real justice (special drug courts)? (1992, November). *National Law Journal, 15*(9).

Research Triangle Institute. (1976). *Drug use and crime: Report of the panel on drug use and criminal behavior*. Springfield, VA: National Technical Information Service.

Rosenbaum, M. (1981). *Women on heroin*. New Brunswick, NJ: Rutgers University Press.

Rosenthal, V., & Shimberg, E. (1958). A program of group therapy with incarcerated narcotic addicts. *Journal of Criminal Law, Criminology and Police Science, 49,* 140-144.

Rossi, P. H., & Freeman, H. E. (1993). *Evaluation: A systematic approach* (5th ed.). Newbury Park, CA: Sage.

Salholz, E. (1989, September 11). Counting trees as the forest burns: Why the experts have been slow to respond to the crack epidemic. *Newsweek, 114,* 26-28.

Sandoz, C. E. (1922, May-June). Report on morphinism to the municipal court of Boston. *Journal of Criminal Law and Criminology, 13.*

Schechter, A., & Polk, K. (1977). *Youth service bureaus, national evaluation program, Phase I assessment*. Washington, DC: Government Printing Office.

Schmidt, C. F. (1960). Urban crime areas: Part II. *American Sociological Review, 25,* 655-678.

Schwartz, R. D., & Skolnick, J. H. (1963). Two studies of legal stigma. *Social Problems, 10,* 138-142.

Scott, W. (1916). *Seventeen years in the underworld*. New York: Abingdon.

Sessions, W. S. (1989). Legalization of drugs—no! *FBI Law Enforcement Bulletin, 58*(2).

Shannon, E. (1989, August 28). Attacking the source: Bennett's plan to send military advisers to aid anti-narcotics campaigns in Peru and Bolivia arouses serious worries in Washington. *Time,* p. 10.

Sharpe, M. C. (1928). *Chicago May*. New York: Macaulay.

Smith, B. E., Davis, R. C., & Goretsky, S. R. (1991). *Strategies for courts to cope with the caseload pressures of drug cases: Final report*. Chicago: American Bar Association, Criminal Justice Section.

Smith, B. E., Davis, R. C., & Goretsky, S. R. (1993). Drug night courts: How feasible are they? Assessing Cook County's example. *Bulletin, 1*(1).

Smith, B. E., Lurigio, A. J., Davis, R. C., Elstein, S. G., & Popkin, S. J. (1994). Burning the midnight oil: An examination of Cook County's night court. In Swift and effective justice: New approaches to drug cases in the states [Special issue]. *Justice System Journal, 17,* 41-52.

Smith, M. H. (1868). *Sunshine and shadow in New York.* Hartford, CT: J. B. Burr.

Soulé, F., Gihan, J. H., & Nisbet, J. (1885). *The annals of San Francisco.* New York: Appleton.

Speaking out: What must be done. (1989, August). *Ebony, 44,* 156.

Stanton, J. M. (1969). *Lawbreaking and drug dependence.* Albany: New York State Division of Parole, Bureau of Research and Statistics.

State of New York Joint Legislative Committee. (n.d.). *Report of the State of New York Joint Legislative Committee* (Legislative Document, Report No. 7). Albany: Author.

Stephens, R. C. (1987). *Mind-altering drugs: Use, abuse, and treatment.* Newbury Park, CA: Sage.

Stephens, R. C., & Cottrell, E. E. (1972). A followup study of 200 narcotic addicts committed for treatment under the Narcotic Addict Rehabilitation Act (NARA). *British Journal of Addiction, 67,* 45-53.

Stephens, R. C., & McBride, D. C. (1976). Becoming a street addict. *Human Organization, 35,* 87-93.

Sterling, E. (1991). What should we do about drugs? Manage the problem through legalization. *Vital Speeches, 57*(20).

Sutherland, E. H. (1937). *The professional thief.* Chicago: University of Chicago Press.

Sykes, G. M. (1965). *The society of captives: A study of a maximum security prison.* New York: Atheneum.

System Sciences. (1979). *Evaluation of treatment alternatives to street crime: National evaluation program, Phase II report.* Washington, DC: National Institute of Law Enforcement and Criminal Justice.

Tauber, J. S. (1993, August). *A judicial primer on unified drug courts and court-ordered drug rehabilitation programs.* Paper presented at the California Continuing Judicial Studies Program, Dana Point, CA.

Tauber, J. S. (1994, February). Drug courts: Treating drug-using offenders through sanctions, incentives. *Corrections Today,* pp. 28-30, 32-33, 76-77.

Terry, C. E., & Pellens, M. (1928). *The opium problem.* New York: Bureau of Social Hygiene.

Thompson, W. G. (1902). *Textbook of practical medicine.* Philadelphia: Lea Brothers.

Toborg, M. A., Levin, D. R., Milkman, R. H., & Center, L. J. (1976). *Treatment Alternatives to Street Crime (TASC) projects: National evaluation program, Phase I summary report.* Washington, DC: National Institute of Law Enforcement and Criminal Justice.

TRB. (1989, October 9). Attitude problem [in From Washington]. *New Republic, 201,* 4, 40.

Trebach, A. S. (1982). *The heroin solution.* New Haven, CT: Yale University Press.

Trebach, A. S., & Englesman, E. (1989). Why not decriminalize? *New Perspectives Quarterly, 6*(2).

Turque, B. (1989, May 29). Why justice can't be done: America's courts and prisons are overwhelmed. *Newsweek, 113,* 36-37.

Uelman, G. F., & Haddox, V. G. (1989). *Drug abuse and the law sourcebook.* New York: Clark Boardman.

U.S. Department of Health, Education and Welfare. (1963). *Narcotic drug addiction* (PHS Publication No. 1021, Health Monograph No. 2). Washington, DC: Government Printing Office.

U.S. Department of Justice, Bureau of Justice Assistance. (1988). *Treatment alternatives to street crime* (Program brief). Washington, DC: Author.

U.S. Department of Justice, Bureau of Justice Statistics. (1989). *Special report.* Washington, DC: Government Printing Office.

U.S. Department of Justice, Federal Bureau of Investigation. (1991). *Uniform crime reports: 1990.* Washington, DC: Government Printing Office.

U.S. Treasury Department, Bureau of Narcotics. (1940). *Traffic in opium and dangerous drugs for the year ended December 31, 1939.* Washington, DC: Government Printing Office.

Viglucci, A. (1992, July 5). More money won't solve jail crowding. *Miami Herald,* p. 1B

Viorst, M. (1979). *Fire in the streets: America in the 1960s.* New York: Simon & Schuster.

Voss, H. L., & Stephens, R. C. (1973). Criminal history of narcotic addicts. *Drug Forum, 2,* 191-202.

Waldman, S. (1989, April 10). Turf wars in the federal bureaucracy: More agencies, money—and confusion. *Newsweek, 113,* 24.

Walsh, G. P. (1981). *Opium and narcotic laws.* Washington, DC: Government Printing Office.

Wentworth, H., & Flexner, S. B. (Eds.). (1960). *Dictionary of American slang.* New York: Thomas Y. Crowell.

Weppner, R. S., & McBride, D. C. (1975). Comprehensive drug programs: The Dade County, Florida example. *Psychiatry, 132,* 734-738.

Werner, J. (1909, June). *The illegal sale of cocaine.* Paper presented at the Sixteenth Annual Meeting of the International Association of Chiefs of Police.

White, G. M. (1907). *From boniface to bank burglar.* New York: Seaboard.

Wice, P. B. (1994, January-February). Making a difference in the war on drugs: A case study of judicial reform and leadership. *Criminal Law Bulletin, 30.*

Wilson, J. Q., & DiIulio, J. J., Jr. (1989, July 10). Crackdown: Treating the symptoms of the drug problem. *New Republic, 201,* 21-25.

Wish, E. D. (1990). Drug testing and the identification of drug using criminals. In J. A. Inciardi (Ed.), *Handbook of drug control in the United States* (pp. 229-244). Westport, CT: Greenwood.

Wood, G. B. (1856). *A treatise on therapeutics and pharmacology or materia medica.* Philadelphia: J. B. Lippincott.

The wrong drug war. (1989, September 25). *The Nation, 249,* 297.

Young, A. W. (1973). Skin complications of heroin addiction: Bullous impetigo. *New York State Journal of Medicine, 73,* 1681-1684.

Zorbaugh, H. W. (1923). *The Gold Coast and the slum.* Chicago: University of Chicago Press.

Cases

Gagnon v. Scarpelli, 411 U.S. 778 (1973).

Linder v. United States, 268 U.S. 5 (1925).

Marshall v. United States, 414 U.S. 417 (1974).

Mempa v. Rhay, 398 U.S. 128 (1967).

Morrissey v. Brewer, 408 U.S. 471 (1972).

People v. Newman, 40 A.D.2d 633, N.Y.S.2d 127 (Sup. Ct. 1973), rev'd 32 N.Y.2d 379, 298 N.E.2d 651, 345 N.Y.S.2d 502 (1973).

Robinson v. California, 370 U.S. 660 (1962).

Schmerber v. California, 384 U.S. 757 (1966).

United States v. Behrman, 258 U.S. 280 (1922).

Webb v. United States, 249 U.S. 96 (1919).

Whipple v. Martinson, 256 U.S. 41, 45 (1921).

Index

About the Authors

James A. Inciardi, Ph.D., is Director of the Center for Drug and Alcohol Studies at the University of Delaware, Professor in the Department of Sociology and Criminal Justice at Delaware, Adjunct Professor in the Department of Epidemiology and Public Health at the University of Miami School of Medicine, and Distinguished Professor at the State University of Rio de Janeiro. He is also a member of the National Academy of Sciences Committee on Opportunities in Substance Abuse Research. During the past few years, he has served as Chair of the NIDA/NIH Drug Abuse/AIDS Research Review Committee and has been a member of the U.S. Sentencing Commission Task Force on Drugs and Violence, the National Academy of Sciences Committee on Substance Abuse and Mental Health Issues in AIDS Research, and the National Safety Council Committee on Alcohol and Other Drugs. He earned his Ph.D. in sociology at New York University and has research, clinical, field, and teaching experience in the areas of AIDS, substance abuse, and criminal justice. He has done extensive research and consulting work both nationally and internationally, and has published 37 books and 190 articles and chapters in the areas of substance abuse, criminology, criminal justice, history, folklore, social policy, AIDS, medicine, and law.

Duane C. McBride, Ph.D., is Professor and Chair of the Behavioral Sciences Department at Andrews University, Chair of the Research Center of the Institute of Alcoholism and Drug Dependency at Andrews, Adjunct Professor in the Department of Epidemiology and Public Health at the University of Miami School of Medicine, and Chair of the NIDA/NIH Drug Abuse/AIDS Research Review Committee. He earned his M.A. in sociology at the University of Maryland and his Ph.D. in sociology at the University of Kentucky. In recent years he has been actively involved in a variety of substance abuse and drugs/crime research projects funded by the National Institute on Drug Abuse and the U.S. Department of Justice, and has published 60 articles, chapters, monographs, and books in the areas of substance abuse, criminology, criminal justice, and AIDS.

James E. Rivers, Ph.D., is Deputy Director of the Comprehensive Drug Research Center at the University of Miami School of Medicine and a Research Associate Professor in both the Department of Sociology and the Department of Epidemiology and Public Health at Miami. He earned his Ph.D. in sociology at the University of Kentucky and has research, teaching, and administrative/policy experience in a broad range of substance abuse areas, including multiagency management information systems and performance evaluation, communitywide prevention and treatment needs assessment, and evaluation studies in the areas of drug abuse treatment and HIV/AIDS prevention/intervention. In recent years he has been Director of the Metropolitan Dade County (Florida) Office of Substance Abuse Control ("drug czar") and Loaned Executive to the Law Enforcement, Courts, and Corrections Task Force of the Miami Coalition for a Safe and Drug Free Community. He has been a consultant to numerous substance abuse and criminal justice organizations, and has published widely in the areas of drug abuse, criminal justice, public policy, management information systems, research methodology, and HIV/AIDS.